To:

Michelle and Richard

With Warmest Regards!

J. Drew Harrington

MY TOWN

April 30, 1994

Printed and Published in the USA By:
Colonial Press
1237 Stevens Road S.E.
Bessemer, AL 35023
(205) 428-2146

Library of Congress Catalog Number: 93-071841

ISBN Number: 1-56883-006-8

MY TOWN

By

J. Drew Harrington

COLONIAL PRESS

PREFACE

No author writes a book by himself. Many people contribute to the effort, even though he might put the words to the paper. In my case there are more people than I can thank, but a few deserve special recognition.

Those individuals whose stories are told on these pages must be thanked. These people touched my life in a very special way.

Jack Venable, editor of THE TALLASSEE TRIBUNE, who took a chance that his readers would read the stories. He was willing to print them without any real personal knowledge of the author.

Thanks beyond my ability to express them go to Elizabeth Jensen, secretary of the History Department. Liz read, edited, corrrected, and made the computer do wonders with my scribbling. She is an indispensable member of the department. Besides Liz, who deserves all the accolades I can bestow upon her, I want to thank the young ladies who typed the mauscript. Since there were many, I must just thank them as a group.

My friend, Carlton Jackson, encouraged me every step of the way. His friendship is irreplaceable.

My deepest and most heartfelt thanks go to my wonderful and loving wife, MARIA GALLINI HARRINGTON. No man ever had a better partner. She works beside me, dreams with me, and always loves me. I can never repay that love, so I dedicate this book to her.

CONTENTS

INTRODUCTION

These are stories of MY TOWN. While they are my stories of MY TOWN, I hope that they will remind you of stories of YOUR TOWN. What makes them my stories and my town are three things, which cannot be controlled by any of us and yet are common to all of us.

First is the fact that none of us can choose our biological parents. When two people decide to produce a new life that embryo has no choice but to be born to those two individuals. For some of us that is a real blessing, but for others it is a curse. It was my good fortune, and I hope yours, to be blessed with a wonderful set of parents.

Second is the fact that our birth is controlled by a time factor over which we have no say. When our parents chose to conceive us is something about which we can do nothing, yet it affects our entire life. We are forced to live in a time frame over which we have no determination. Events which

1

occur during our life will shape us, since we must live within that time frame. Because of that my stories about MY TOWN are fixed within the span of time in which I existed in it, just as yours are controlled by the time in which you spent in your town.

Finally, we cannot choose the place of our birth. When the time of our birth arrives, it will occur whether our mother is in a hospital room, a stable, a taxi, or wherever. Furthermore, for several years of our life we have no control over where we live since we are the responsibility of our parents until we are able to fend for ourselves.

Having made these statements, let me point out that the stories contained in this book are my personal stories about my life in MY TOWN, but that they are stories which are common to all of us. Therefore, I hope that each of you will find in them something with which you can identify. I hope that they will bring to mind some fond memories and maybe a few chuckles. Since life is not lived in small compartments, it is difficult to categorize my stories although I have tried to group them in some order of subject. Some refuse to be so neatly catalogued, so I list some at the end as miscellaneous. After inviting you to visit MY TOWN, I introduce you to some of my teachers and school experiences, to some people who live in it, to some of its institutions, and then I tell about some events that occurred, some of my animal pets, and the games we played. I am sure that many of the people, things, games, and events will remind you of experiences from your own life.

LET'S VISIT

In <u>The Adventures of Tom Sawyer</u>, Mark Twain, in "A Missouri Maiden's Farewell to Alabama," described the physical location of what was to become MY TOWN with these words: "Have roamed and read near Tallapoosa's stream; Have listened to Tallassee's warring floods, And Wooed on Coosa's side Aurora's beam."

Many years after Samuel Clemens wrote those words, pilots in the United State Air Force called it, "The Town of the White Roofs," because of the white-gray asbestos shingles of the houses of the mill village.

Physically, MY TOWN sits astride the Tallapoosa River, about fifty winding miles upstream from Montgomery, but MY TOWN which I want you to visit with me is not the town which rests on that geographical location today; that town belongs to another people and another generation.

4

You see, Thomas Wolfe, an American novelist, wrote, "You cannot go home again;" while an ancient Greek philosopher, Heraclitus, said, "You cannot step into the same river twice." With those thoughts in mind, I want to invite you to visit MY TOWN, which lived on the site fifty or so years ago and which still lives on in my mind.

MY TOWN was a mill town, a textile town. The vast majority of people who lived in and around MY TOWN were employees of the mill company in the truest sense. Most workers lived in company houses, traded at the company store, sent their kids to company schools, and depended upon company doctors, dentists, and the company hospital to take care of them and their families. The company even sponsored a local library to broaden the minds of those kids interested enough to make the trip to check out books.

Besides being a typical mill town, MY TOWN was very much a southern town, distinctly divided along racial lines. There was a mill village for the Blacks, which was separated from that of the Whites. While they associated in the mill, where Blacks and Whites worked side-by-side in certain areas, no social relationships existed outside the work place.

Even with this description of MY TOWN, you cannot really get to know it unless you come to meet and know its character. No town is really anything without the people who live in it. I want to introduce you to many of the characters and events which made MY TOWN. Some are comical characters, others are serious characters, and still others are thoughtful. Some of the events in their lives are amusing, some charming, and some are tragic; but all are interesting. With these thoughts, I invite you to come and visit MY TOWN and its people.

SCHOOL AND TEACHERS

All of us experienced that first day of school. For many that day either made or broke our desire for learning. I was lucky in that my early school experience instilled a love for learning in me. Events of those early years still linger fondly in my memory. I want to share some of those memories which are sure to kindle some fond thoughts of your own early school days. Those days would have been meaningless without the teachers, so I would like to acquaint you with some of those elementary and high school teachers who meant so much to me and who I hope will cause you to think of some teachers who were special to you.

FIRST GRADE - FIRST DAY

No experience can be as upsetting to a youngster as that momentous occasion when he or she has to dress up in those new clothes which have been bought with money saved just for that purpose and has to trudge off to school for the very fist time.

If doctors could only measure the increase in heartbeat that occurs in those frightened little bodies, they might decide it was cause for educational reform. At any rate, if there is no permanent damage to the heart of the child, there certainly is a change in the child's psyche. Nowadays with pre-school programs the experience is lessened, but my first day and first grade experience left a mark that remains.

For six years, I had lived in the loving and tender protection of a family that saw to all of my needs, not necessarily all of my wants; however, I had been fed, clothed, entertained, and even cuddled a few times. I had been free

8

to rise and play from sun-up to sunset and even a few times after sundown.

As I neared the age of six, I became interested enough in the comics to try to learn to read. I often wonder why educators spend so much time and money trying to develop attractive and colorful books when the comics prove just as effective. At any rate, I shall always be thankful to "Ole Grandma" (The Montgomery Advertiser) for providing me with my first reading tools.

As I entered the fall of my sixth year, I sensed that something was changing. Mother had carefully seen to the purchase of new pants and overalls as well as a pair of new shoes. These were not Sunday clothes, so my little mind became suspicious. Finally, that big day in September arrived. Mother dressed me in a pair of new pants, a new shirt, my new shoes, and tried to comb down my rooster tail, my trade-mark. Off we trudged toward that fearsome building known as the "little school," to contrast it from the "high school" which sat next to it.

The first thing that struck me as I walked into the assigned classroom was the look of horror on the faces of all those scrubbed kids that I had been playing in the dirt with only yesterday. I could hardly believe my eyes at the transformation. If someone had shouted, "BOO!", there would have been thirty young deaths at that moment.

My teacher, a nice middle-aged lady, began to get the necessary information from my mother as well as from the mothers of my soon-to-be classmates. This activity took most of an hour and a half. When that chore was accomplished, we were in for a surprise because our teacher stood and said, "Class, your mothers are now going to leave you."

Now to a six year old child, those words can be bone-chilling, for he or she has no sense of time and to say, "Your mother is going to leave you," can almost cause heart failure. At any rate, the reaction was spontaneous--massive squalling from about three-fourths of the class. Nonetheless, out walked the moms as though in protest for having to put up with those brats for six years. The sight of one's mother walking away at one of the greatest crises in life can send chills up one's spine. I was probably one of those who cried.

The rest of the day was spent in trying to adjust to a change in my life which was to have a permanent effect on it. My first grade teacher proved to be a person who knew the fears of little girls and boys and how to calm them. Nevertheless, the first day of the first grade marks a child for life. The rest of the year left its imprint also.

FIRST GRADE - THE YEAR

I lived through that frightening first day of school. If I thought that was an experience, the remainder of the year had a few more surprises for me.

Life did settle down after the first week. I found that I did not have to come dressed as neatly as I had the first day. I soon was wearing my clean and comfortable overalls along with the homemade shirts which my mother had made from printed flour sacks. All in all it was not too bad to dress to go to school.

I quickly developed a pattern which was to remain with me through school and into later life. I arose, dressed, ate breakfast, and soon as I could I would hurry to school. I found that one could get anywhere from thirty minutes to an hour of free play time, if one came to school that early. I vowed never to be late if I could help it.

A gang of us boys would arrive early and break out our sack of marbles. It was a point of pride to see who had the prettiest marbles and the best aggies. Every boy had his favorite "taw" or shooter. As a matter of fact, one rule which we all had to obey was that no one could use a steel marble as a "taw"; it just did too much damage to the smaller glass marbles.

Another point of pride was to bring your marbles in a Prince Albert tobacco can. If you could not find a can, then you had to stick with a tobacco sack or a homemade one, if you could convince your mother that she should save your honor by making it.

Besides marbles, the boys loved to play with their toy cars and trucks. Since there was a lot of dirt available in the schoolyard, it was not hard for us to find enough to cut roads and to build hills over which to race our toys. We spent many a happy hour pushing toy cars and trucks over those ruts. Notice that I said pushing, for our toys had no batteries to cause them to run automatically.

As a matter of fact, I can remember the first self-propelled toy which I saw. It was during the first grade that a classmate secured from "Santa Claus" at a Christmas party about which I shall write later. The toy was a caterpillar which was wound with a key and operated by a spring inside. It became the envy of the first grade boys.

Three things stand out about the remainder of the first grade. Besides our regular book work and learning skills, our teacher decided that we should draw and color Thanksgiving pictures. This experience turned me against art and has affected my outlook on painting ever since. Here is what happened.

I had drawn the typical picture of the pilgrim, the turkey, and the pumpkin. In trying to color the picture, my teacher suggested that I outline it in black. Now what I did not realize was that she wanted me to outline the black objects in black and the others in their own color. Do you realize what a shock it can be to a first grader who thought he was following instructions to have a teacher almost go into hysterics as she looks at his black outlined picture? I have never liked coloring or painting since.

The second major event was the Monday following a peaceful weekend in December. We returned to school after a weekend of typical childhood play, but there was a different atmosphere--a more somber one. It meant very little to me at the time, but I was told that the Japanese had bombed some place called Pearl Harbor.

The major changes I noticed the next few weeks and months were an increase in the time my mother and father worked, the number of young men who seemed to disappear from MY TOWN, and the strange new comic strips that had foreign looking people and names in them. War is hell and it sure changed MY TOWN.

Finally, I lost my first grade teacher, even before I had a chance to really get to know her. She left in mid-year to start her own school in another town. So at mid-year, I had to break in a new teacher, which proved not to be too hard and earned me a friend for life. The first grade can be hard on a kid.

UNREQUITED LOVE

Sir Lancelot had his Guinevere, Dante idolized Beatrice, and Charlie Brown's friend tries to find the name of the little girl in his class so that he can send her a Christmas card and later a Valentine's card. Like these famous characters, I had my unrequited love. I identify with the character in Peanuts, since my unrequited love was a first grade classmate. To appreciate the degree to which that unrequited love has haunted me, you must understand my early childhood.

I grew up in a neighborhood with several girls and I also had a sister. Now in our preschool days, we played together as equals. I never paid any attention to the young girls as anything but playmates. They could hit the ball as hard as any of us boys; they could run faster than some of us; and they could climb trees much better than most of us. Most importantly, they could fight with the best of us. Who could have romantic ideas about girls like that?

Finally, the day came that I was to start school for the first time. While my sister had to wait another year, one of the girls in my neighborhood, Jean Claire Hall, did begin school with me. I never thought of her other than as a tomboy playmate.

For the first month of school the boys tried to pretend that the girls did not exist, except as objects of their scorn. By the second month, some of the boys had begun to talk with the girls rather than pick at them. By the third month, it was quite evident that girls were more than butts of our pranks. Since the rest of the boys began eyeing certain girls, I decided that I had better find one that I could like.

As I said I had known all of the girls in my neighborhood, but when I enrolled in school I found there were other girls whom I did not know. Now most of the neighborhood girls had either blond or brunette hair. Much to my surprise and delight there was one pretty young girl with red hair and green eyes in my class. That young girl became the object of my attention, but I tried to act cool and not let anyone know it.

Being shy, I tried to concoct ways to be near her. When there was a reading session, I would try to get a table with her. During science projects, I tried to get the teacher to team me with her. I was always ready to help her with her math. Despite all of my efforts she hardly gave me the time of day. The more my love remained unrequited, the deeper I fell.

Finally, one Monday morning, after I roamed the fall woods picking the last of the wild flowers, I came to school with my gift of love for her. I waited at the front door, but she did not come. At last the bell rang and we all had to go to class. Still she did not show up. As roll was called the teacher came to her name and said that she had moved away from MY TOWN. My heart stopped for my love was gone and like Charlie Brown's friend I never learned her name.

With the haunting that comes only to those with an unrequited love, I peer deeply into the eyes of every woman with red hair and green eyes that I meet. My love with the red hair has become my Beatrice.

16

CLASS ASSIGNMENTS

Every August the kids in MY TOWN looked forward to the first week's newspaper because it contained two vital pieces of information that would affect their lives for the coming school year. That issue contained the names of the teachers for the upcoming term and a list of books which were to be used in the various classes for that year.

The first item was very important since there were about two teachers for each of the elementary grades. Because the school board divided the pupils into two as nearly equal parts as they could, those of us who had last names that began with a letter near the middle of the alphabet were particularly interested in seeing how we had been placed for the coming term.

As one might suspect there were teachers whom we wanted to avoid at all costs, and unless the school officials switched by changing the teacher who usually got a certain part of the alphabet or unless there was an influx of new students, we could pretty well tell our fate. Nonetheless, the

17

element of uncertainty remained so we eagerly awaited the annual issue of the newspaper. This became even more important after we moved from the sixth to the seventh grade, since the students for the school in EAST MY TOWN came to the high school in MY TOWN. This really rearranged the set distribution of students who had been together for six years, but it made life more interesting as we made new friends and enemies.

The second item in the annual issue of the newspaper set off a treasure hunt for several weeks, many times lasting until after school started. In those days, there was no such thing as a free textbook. Furthermore, unless your parents were extremely wealthy, you were encouraged to find used textbooks for your classes, which necessitated the treasure hunt.

You and your parents tried to think of kids who already had passed the classes you were scheduled to take and you contacted them about selling you their used textbooks. Many times you would think of a person, contact that individual, only to learn that some other student had just beaten you to purchase the desired text. That meant that you had to go looking elsewhere.

As I look back on this system, I ponder several things. One is that although I am sure that it was a financial burden on the parents, I do not remember any case of a student not being able to have a book. Another is that the system of our hunting our used texts caused us to develop a sense of friendship which in a sense put all of us who used the same text year after year in a sort of ancestral line. As one might guess, we took pride in those texts and tried to see that they were as well preserved as possible.

I sometimes wonder about free texts where the student has no sense of responsibility for the property; signing a piece of paper saying that your parents are responsible just does not make the impact that a search for a text does.

JIM

One of the highlights of each school year occurred when each room of each grade in the elementary school had to present a play at an assembly of the other classes. Few of them stick in my mind, but two are rather vivid. One is when I was in the first grade and in the operetta. I had to play a bumblebee. I will never forget the effort my mother put into getting that costume and its wire wings together. All of that effort went toward seeing her son glide across the stage for about a minute or less; he did not even have a speaking part and he certainly could not sing.

The other play is more delightful to recall. I think it was in the sixth grade that my class was called upon to put on its annual play. Our teacher chose TOM SAWYER as the production to be presented to the class. I doubt there is a young boy alive who has not dreamed of being like Tom Sawyer. When it was announced that our class would be doing TOM SAWYER, every boy in the class immediately visualized himself as the charming con-artist Tom. At last, I would get a chance to show my classmates that I could do more than glide across a stage as a bumblebee. When tryouts were held, it became quite evident that another kid in the class would be cast in the coveted role. Never one to admit total defeat, I regrouped and thought of other roles. While I was plotting for another role, my teacher was thinking of me in the role of Jim, Tom's Black sidekick. It was not exactly the role I wanted but I respected my teacher so much that when she insisted that I read for it, I did. Thus I became Jim.

The first production of the play was put on the for the grade school audience. Tom's and my big scene was the whitewashing of the fence. Tom, who was played by John Herren (I think), came across as a most clever con-artist and before I realized it he had me painting the fence. We must have done well for the principal asked us to give another performance at the high school assembly. We did and again

20

the entire cast of the play proved to be delightful which made our teacher and principal happy.

As we presented the play, I realized one advantage that I had gained by being cast as Jim. I had to have stage make-up put on my white skin to make me look brown as a Black boy. Since it had to be applied to my hands and face, it was impossible for me to clean up at school, so I was allowed to leave school and leisurely (at least I took my time whatever the plan of the school officials was) go home and wash the make-up from my hands and face. I was the only one of the cast that had the opportunity to legally cut school on two occasions. Jim has always remained my favorite character in TOM SAWYER.

A footnote for those of you who have not read TOM SAWYER for a long time. Tallassee is mentioned in the novel. In the Missouri maiden's "A Farewell To Alabama," she describes the falls at Tallassee.

THE TOURNAMENT

I never picked up a basketball until I was in the seventh grade. As a youngster I had always played with a football, softball, or baseball. I am sure that basketball had been played in MY TOWN for many years, but it did not receive the attention the other sports did.

When I was in the ninth grade, someone decided that we needed a junior varsity team in MY TOWN. Mr. Robert Saunders was asked to coach the team. Twelve of us boys tried out for the team. Now I must confess that I was not and never will be any good at basketball, but I tried a hard as anyone on the team. I was so bad that at times Coach Saunders would scrimmage with nine men rather than let me on the floor, which gives you a picture of my athletic ability on a basketball court.

The powers-that-be decided that there should be a county-wide junior high basketball tournament and that MY

TOWN should host it. When Coach Saunders told us about it, we were ecstatic. My enthusiasm soon diminished when he said that there could only be ten boys on the squad. Although one boy had quit, which cut the number to eleven, I realized that I probably would be dropped. However, as fate would have it, Coach Saunders decided to let William Guiliford and me draw for the tenth spot. I have never won a lottery nor many prizes, but that win of the draw was the best surprise of my young life. Little did I know the penalty which I would pay for that drawing. Some of the team who had not wanted me to play tried to get Coach Saunders to change his mind, but he refused.

I had been so sure that I would not make the team that I had not brought my tennis shoes to school that day. That afternoon in practice I borrowed Coach Saunders's shoes. Now one would think that a coach would have bigger feet than a ninth grader, that was not the case. His shoes were a size too small for me, however I wanted so badly to play that I bent my toes under so that I could practice. This worked for a time, but once down the floor I forgot and stopped suddenly. I felt the pain as my left toenail was torn from my toe and bent straight up. I continued with the pain and practice only to go charging down the floor and to another sudden stop with the results that my right toenail was also torn loose. That night when I went to bed I had to sleep without any cover and on my back since my toenails were so sore.

Determined to play in the tournament, I taped my torn toenails down and continued to play with my own shoes. We won most of our games by rather large scores so I got to play quite a bit. In the last game (I had not scored the entire tournament), in desperation I threw up an off-balance shot that went into the bucket. I would have traded a dozen toenails for those two points.

ON THE BENCH AND BUS

Following my short-lived career on the basketball court in junior high, I was convinced by the coach of the varsity team to become his manager and score-keeper. I was thrilled with the job since I got to travel with the team and to be a part of the basketball program. I especially enjoyed the role as the coach's right hand man. The role also gave me a chance to see the pressure under which a coach has to work. At times parents jumped him for not playing their son as often as they felt he should. At other times he had to discipline players and their parents attacked him for not letting their sons play. At other times people blamed him for losing games when he was forced for disciplinary reasons to bench some of his best players. I remember two incidents related to my role as manager and scorekeeper.

Once we were playing Lanett and when the end of the game came, my book was two points off from the scorer's book, my team had lost the game by one point and since the two points which I had recorded would mean the reversal of the score, a meeting was held between the scorers, the referees, and the coaches. Luckily, I had been keeping a shot chart as well as the record book. I was able to go back through and show the referees where the official scorer had made a two point error and my team was awarded the victory.

The other incident had to do with a person whom I have counted as a friend since those high school days in MY TOWN. Since I did not play, I was constantly kidded by the members of the team. Most of the time it was good natured kidding, but one night as we were preparing to make a trip to Selma I did something that gave the guys an opportunity to tease me. They did in a rather merciless way. As the kidding got really bad Gene Langford spoke up on my behalf. He turned the criticism around and made the fellows realize how cruel they were being toward me. All of a sudden, they stopped because Gene had shamed them. I never appreciated anyone any more than I did Gene on that night. He became a fast friend whom I shall never forget. He taught me what true friendship is about.

THE TEACHERAGE

It was a stately old frame house which stood across the street from the school building. From mid-June until mid-August, it stood empty, but in mid-August it came alive with a bevy of young and not-so-young ladies who were to serve as the mentors of the kids in MY TOWN. This building that housed so much learning and an equal amount of beauty was called "The Teacherage." Most towns have a "Parsonage," but MY TOWN also had its "Teacherage."

This situation was brought about by the board of education's policy which stated that no married woman could teach in the schools of MY TOWN. Because of that policy, the mill company furnished a house for all of the young and not-so-young teachers to live in during the school year.

I often wondered why the board of education adopted this policy. It could have been that they did not want to have to furnish any teacher with maternity leave or it could have been that they did not want to expose those tender minds of ours to pregnant women as teachers; either way it made for an interesting youth, being educated by women who would come into MY TOWN for the school year and be gone during the summer months.

The arrangement seemed to be that the school would furnish the pay for the teachers and they in turn would pay a minimal rent for a room in "The Teacherage." I assume that it worked well for the young ladies did not have to get out in the community to hunt a place to live. Furthermore, it was a very handy place for them, since they would only have to walk across the street to be in their classrooms.

They did have the privacy of their own room, although some shared a large room with another person. They had a common dining area where they would be served breakfast and dinner, if they chose. They would eat their noon meal at the cafeteria with us students.

I often wondered how the superintendent of schools managed to recruit these ladies to come and teach in a school where they were required to live in a rooming house. I suppose that it would be similar to their having lived in a dormitory at college and it certainly removed any doubts as to where they would be living or whether they would have a place to live.

Each year those of us who were students would wait for the list of teachers to be printed to see who the new ones were and who had been in MY TOWN the year before but who would not be returning. If we got a chance, before school started, we would sneak by the "Teacherage" to try to get a look at the new faces and guess as to who might get whom as a teacher.

As students all of us held that rather imposing frame building in awe, since it housed those who were most directly responsible for our well-being during the school year.

TEACHERS

No group of people, except maybe one's parents, plays a greater role in a person's life than one's teachers. I have been extremely blessed with the teachers in my life. I remember most of them and all of them for a different reason.

In the first grade I had Miss Stella Patterson for one semester and Mrs. Wilson Patterson for the second. Miss Ruth Zigler was my second grade teacher. When it came time to start the third grade I went to Miss Zigler's room and refused to go to Miss Mildred Duke's room for the third grade. She became the first teacher on whom I had a crush. She was the most gentle and caring woman I have ever met. I remember her chastising us boys for playing "keeps" with our marbles. She made us promise never to do that again and I promised. I still hold her as a dear friend and wonderful person. For months now I have tried to recall who my fourth grade teacher was but I draw a blank. Miss Lovie Maddox was my fifth grade teacher. I remember how happy I was when I learned that I had not drawn Miss Evelyn King as that teacher. I remember that I put Frederica Dobbs's pigtails in the ink well on my desk and Miss Maddox became very upset with me. Another gentle woman and one of my favorite teachers was the young Miss McNair. I really do not remember her Christian name. She too had a winsome way with her students.

Junior high school brought the first multiplicity of teachers during one year. My seventh grade homeroom teacher was Miss Ancille Riggs. I remember that she talked my Dad into giving our class a young pig to be raffled off at the annual fall festival at school. I also remember that she had a 1937 Ford which she named Pheidippides because it ran so slowly. She must have figured that Pheidippides made it to Sparta and back to Athens about as fast as her car would run. Little did I know that I would spend each semester for the remainder of my life talking about that Athenian runner. It was in the seventh grade that I had my first male teacher, Mr. Stewart, whom we promptly named "Bull Moose" because of his size. Another favorite of mine was Miss Ruth Coker, my eighth grade homeroom teacher. She taught me never to promise anything which I could not deliver. I have always tried to remember that advice. Mrs.

Virginia Golden, a widow, was my ninth grade homeroom and literature teacher. She was allowed to teach because she was a widow. She also taught French which I took. I remember one literature test where she had put several characters from our reading to be identified. I got all of them but Elizabeth Blackwell and I had to sit there and recreate every story and every character until it finally came to me that she was the first woman to attend medical school. I have never forgotten her. Miss Vernelle Stokes served as my eleventh grade homeroom teacher. I will save the two ladies who served as my senior teachers for a future column since they played such an important role in my life.

There have been times when I thought I would like to have had some better teachers, but I never thought that about the teachers I had in MY TOWN. They were first rate and I received a good education from them.

MISS DUKE

The beginning of my third school year held little hope for me. I had learned to enjoy my second grade classmates and teacher. When I showed up for the third grade, I immediately went to the room where I had spent the previous year. My second grade teacher told me that I would have to go to the auditorium for my new class assignment.

As all of the elementary students gathered in the auditorium of the "little school house," I joined them to await whatever fate had in store for me. I listened attentively as the principal assigned the first grade students to their rooms. As he began calling the second grade class, my ears perked up, although I knew that I had passed to the third grade. When he called my name, the principal stated that I was to be in Miss Mildred Duke's room. I did not know Miss Duke and I wanted the security of my previous teacher, so only reluctantly did I follow as she led the class to its new home.

As we got settled into our new surroundings, Miss Duke made us feel that we were her children. It was only a couple of days before I came to realize what a very special woman I had for a teacher. When one of us would become frightened, Miss Duke was always there to quieten our fear. If we became too noisy, she was quick to silence us. When a couple of us would get into fisticuffs, she would separate us and lecture us on the foolishness of settling our differences with our fists. If one of her pupils should fall and hurt himself or herself, Miss Duke provided the tender loving care to make the hurt go away.

I remember Miss Duke for two special reasons. She taught me to enjoy reading. Until the third grade I had been an average reader who preferred playing to sitting still and reading. Miss Mildred Duke taught me the joy and pleasure that can be found within the covers of great pieces of literature. The other lesson came a bit harder, but it has stuck with me throughout my life. One day a group of us boys were playing marbles during our recess period. For some reason we decided to play for "keeps," which meant that whoever won the others's marbles kept them. I am not sure, but I would not be surprised that I became the loser and went to cry to Miss Duke about the loss of my marbles. She called all of us boys together and calmly lectured us about gambling, which is what she considered our playing for "keeps" to be. She made all of us return each others marbles. To this day I have never forgotten that lesson.

In all of my school years I never came across a woman whom I loved more dearly and fondly than Miss Mildred Duke. She broke my young heart when she decided to get married, but she has remained a wonderful and dear friend.

MRS. COKER

My eighth grade teacher was Mrs. R. H. Coker, the widow of one of MY TOWN'S most famous physicians. Dr. Coker had died rather unexpectedly in the 1930s and Mrs. Coker had to take a job teaching to be able to raise her two daughters. Over the years she had become one of the best loved teachers in MY TOWN'S school.

Mrs. Coker was a small woman with gray hair and a quick smile. She taught what is known today as the language arts. In her class we learned grammar, spelling, and studied literature. She had a manner about her that made each student want to do his or her best.

I remember two incidents about my eighth grade class with Mrs. Coker. At that age, we boys were getting to the point of noticing girls as something other than a bother. Now I was as bashful as I could be about girls. I was having a hard time screwing up my courage to ask a certain young lady in the class to accompany me to a basketball game. I made the mistake of telling other boys about my plan and they began to tease me unmercifully. Since the young lady and I both were in Mrs. Coker's class, one day when she was out of the room the guys started teasing both of us. About the time that they were at their wildest, Mrs. Coker came back into the room. She immediately began to calm the class down. After quiet had been resumed, she gave all of us a lecture on courtesy. From that time forward I did not receive any teasing about girls as long as I was in Mrs. Coker's room.

When one of us would ask Mrs. Coker about doing something for us, she would always answer that she would not promise but that she would try to do it if she could. It struck me funny that she would never make a promise, so one day I asked her why she always qualified her answer about aiding someone. She replied that she was not always sure that she could keep a promise so rather than disappoint someone she would agree to try but she would never promise. For some reason that struck me as a good advice. I have tried to follow it since then. I will do anything I can for a person, but I am reluctant to promise.

For years after I left MY TOWN I would return, and each time I would visit Mrs. Coker. It is odd how the little things that teachers do often make the most impact upon students.

MRS. GOLDEN

Mrs. Virginia Noble Golden was one of my favorite teachers. She was a widow who had lost her husband in World War II and she taught English Literature and Latin. The year before I was eligible to take Latin, the officials at school decided there was not enough demand, so they asked Mrs. Golden to teach two years of French. She agreed willingly and so instead of Latin, which I had to learn later, I took two years of French with Mrs. Golden.

Not only did Mrs. Golden teach literature and French, she also wrote A HISTORY OF TALLASSEE. As a celebration of its anniversary, the Mount Vernon Woodbury Mills commissioned Mrs. Golden to write the history and they had it published. The company then distributed a copy of it to every mill hand who was working at that time as well as to those who had retired. Although it is dated now, it remains one of the best histories of Tallassee. Donald Warren and I became involved with this history book because when the company decided to distribute them to each household, the officials asked the school officials to select two young men to do the distributing. Donald and I were selected and so we missed several days of school to earn some money by distributing the books.

There are two stories about Mrs. Golden's literature class that I remember vividly. Once in our literature book, we had to read a story about a young French boy who hated to go to school. One day as he slowly dallied about reaching the school, he noticed something was different. As he topped the hill and looked down into the valley where the school was located, he saw a different flag flying from the flagpole. Entering the school he found that his regular teacher had been replaced by a young officer wearing a Nazi uniform. Too late school began to take on a new meaning for him. I do not remember the name of the story nor the author, but the message made a deep impact upon me.

The other incident relates to a test which Mrs. Golden gave to us. She listed several characters from our reading and we were to identify them. I managed to get all of them except one. Since I had gotten the others so quickly I had time to think. I went through every story and each character until I was able to identify Elizabeth Blackwell. As long as I live, I will always remember that the first woman doctor was named Elizabeth Blackwell.

MISSES GIBSON AND HAYNES

No two women affected more young people in MY TOWN than Miss Mildred Gibson and Miss Sarah Haynes. These two ladies were teachers at the high school in MY TOWN for as long as I can remember. They had taught there all during my grade school experience and for years after I left MY TOWN.

Miss Mildred Gibson served as junior and senior English teacher. Almost every student who graduated from high school had to have her as a teacher at some point. I remember several events that relate to my English classes with her. First, we nicknamed her "Granny" Gibson, which was a term of endearment for those of us who loved her but of derision for those who despised her. Either way, no one had the nerve to call her "Granny" to her face. Another incident took place in her junior English class where she had us reading poetry. I had grown up knowing what "baloney" was all my life, but when I came to the word "bologna" in a poem I had no earthly or unearthly idea of how to pronounce it. I made some stupid attempt and Miss Gibson thought I was being smart and jumped on me like a jay bird on a junebug. I quickly learned that "bologna" was what I thought was "baloney." In that same English class, Charles Bates was reading a poem in which the word "dewdrops" appeared, but he read it, in my presence and that of the whole class, as "drewdrops." That brought uncontrollable laughter from the class and a stern rebuke from Miss Gibson.

Miss Haynes taught government and civics as well as Alabama history. Most students thought that she was an extremely hard teacher and avoided her. She did have a serious expression on her face most of the time, but she was one of the kindest and most gentle women that I had ever known. It was in her government class in the early fifties that I learned to study and look at all sides of an issue. It was at that time that the country was hit with the "Red Scare" and most high schools would not allow students to have or to read a book on communism. Miss Haynes suggested that we could not fight it if we did not know what it taught, so she encouraged us to read and study it. She took the same approach with all the issues she discussed.

Miss Gibson and Miss Hayes served as senior class sponsors for as many years as I can remember. I still have my senior copy of MY TOWN'S high school newspaper with their picture. They took each senior class and treated the students as members of their own family. They inspired us to reach beyond ourselves and attempt great things. They told us that we could be whatever we wanted to be. They and we felt they were teaching us the American way--to set high goals and work hard to achieve them. My thanks go to these two wonderful teachers; may their tribe increase for the present students need them.

MEN TEACHERS

During my school days, except for coaches, administrators and shop teachers, the board of education in its infinite wisdom chose to hire only female teachers. Even the lady teachers could not be married. It was, therefore, a shock when I encountered my first man teacher outside the areas mentioned above.

When we returned from our holidays during the seventh grade, we found that a new science teacher had been hired to replace ours. I never knew the reason, but I do remember the startled look on our faces as we entered the room and this huge man stood at the front. He introduced himself as Mr. Stewart. Because of his size, we immediately nicknamed him "Bullmoose." After a few weeks we adjusted to him and really enjoyed the rest of the semester. It was a disappointment to some of us when he did not return the next fall.

By the time I reached the tenth grade the school board had hired another man teacher for the social studies position in the eighth and ninth grades. He was Jim Strong. He had served in World War II and had lost one of his legs. Despite that fact, Mr. Strong had a most pleasant personality and even those of us who did not have him for a class came to know and like him. He became an instant hit with the boys of the high school. Since he was unmarried at the time, he was always buddying around with the older boys. On more than one occasion, he was instrumental in playing tricks on students. Besides being a good teacher, his personality made him one of the best liked teachers in our school.

Robert Saunders, who went on to become Dr. Robert Saunders, was my tenth grade science teacher and my junior varsity basketball coach. I suppose having Mr. Saunders for a science teacher was as good an experience as a student at my school could have. He was as knowledgeable about science as anyone that I had ever met. He knew how to keep us interested in the subject. It was not as a science teacher that I remember Mr. Saunders, but as a basketball coach. There had been a move on in the county to establish a junior varsity basketball league among the schools in the county. Not being able to relieve the varsity coaches to handle the squad, the administration prevailed upon Mr. Saunders to take the job. I went out for the team, although I had never handled a basketball until I was in the seventh grade. We started with twelve people on the squad, but by the tournament time only eleven members remained. Since he could field only a ten man team in the tournament, Mr.

Saunders had William Guiliford and me flip a coin to see who stayed. I won and played a most undistinguished tournament. Years later when I had earned my graduate degrees, Dr. Saunders wrote to congratulate me. I could not resist a note thanking him and reminding him that he of all people should know my obstinacy and determination!

DR. NELSON

Probably no one had a greater impact on education in MY TOWN than Dr. Byron B. Nelson. From my very earliest memories, he was connected with the schools of MY TOWN. By the time I was big enough to go to school he had become Superintendent of Schools.

When I first started to school, Mr. Nelson had not earned his Doctor of Education degree. He would spend the summers in a distant place called Nashville, Tennessee, working on his degree. All of the teachers at school admired him for his dedication. I remember once when Miss Mildred Gibson commented to me that Mr. Nelson would always read his textbooks as he rode the bus across town in Nashville. I was impressed at the habit and I have since learned to imitate Dr. Nelson in that respect. I seldom ever travel anywhere without a book to read.

For much of my time in school, Dr. Nelson employed Mr. Clyde Pruitt as principal of the schools. The two of them made a fine pair. Mr. Pruitt appeared as the large grandfatherly type man who could be stern when he had to and Dr. Nelson gave the appearance of a stern man who had few light moments while on school grounds. As students we wanted to stay away from the principal's office, but being summoned to Dr. Nelson's office was the sentence of death. It was to be avoided at all costs.

Dr. Nelson was responsible for bringing some of the finest teachers that I have ever had to MY TOWN. He worked very hard to bring energetic, highly trained, and friendly teachers to educate the young people in the system. I often wondered where he was able to locate such caliber of teachers and how he was able to persuade them to stay on what must have been extremely poor salaries.

Although Dr. Nelson appeared stern, he was one of the most gracious individuals that I have ever met. As I grew older I had occasion to be involved with him in activities outside the confines of school. I found him always to be helpful and generous with his time as well as being constantly encouraging.

After I graduated and left MY TOWN, I came to appreciate what Dr. Byron B. Nelson, whom we secretly and lovingly called "Butterbean Nelson," had done for the education of the young people in MY TOWN. I came to realize that he had been the driving force behind the school system and that although it was not the biggest in the state, those of us who had been educated in it had received an education comparable to that of any other system. My thanks go to Dr. Byron B. Nelson for seeing that we got off on the right foot!

MR. PRUITT

I do not remember when Mr. Clyde Pruitt became principal of the schools in MY TOWN. I only remember that he was a big man with a big frame which contained a lot of muscle. He stood well over six feet and wore glasses. He had a voice that rivaled the rumbling of an erupting volcano and a stare that would wilt a pine tree. Even so, he was a gentle man. The other thing that I remember about his coming to MY TOWN was that he brought with him his teenage daughter, Kitty. She was a very attractive girl and all of the boys her age swarmed around her as though they were bees and she was the queen bee.

As I went through high school, I got to know Mr. Pruitt and to understand what a terrific human being he really was. Three incidents stand out in my mind.

Once when I was a seventh grader I made some smart alec remarks to an older boy who was a husky football player (I was not the most brilliant kid in the world) who rode my bus and cuffed me around pretty good. When I got home, crying as you might expect, the boy's hand prints were still pretty evident on my red face. My parents became angry and called Mr. Pruitt to complain. He promised them that he would look into the matter.

The next morning the football player and I were summoned to the principal's office. If there was any place in school that I hated to go to, it was that office. Mr. Pruitt demanded that we both tell our side of the story. Each told it to put himself in the best light. I am sure that I thought Mr Pruitt would side with a helpless little seventh grader against a strapping football player. With the wisdom of Solomon he scolded us both for acting so childishly and made us shake hands and make up. He warned us not to let it happen again.

The second incident occurred on a beautiful spring morning as I strolled down the hall between classes. I assume that I was caught up on the beauty of the season because I was whistling as I wandered down the hall to my

46

next class. I heard a voice say, "Where do you think you are? On some creek bank or behind a plow in a field?" I turned to see Mr. Pruitt and blushing with embarrassment I promised him that I would stop whistling.

The last episode shows the heart of the man. One day I was asked by the Diversified Occupations teacher to leave school early and to go to his house to assist him in preparing a barbecue for the D.O. Club. I naively assumed that he had cleared it with the office. I also forgot that I had a responsible position on the traffic patrol directing bus traffic after school. I left without getting a replacement. As luck would have it, Mr. Pruitt came to my post and found me missing. He had to fill in for me.

The next day I was summoned to the principal's office, chastised, and was told that I was suspended from school until I had my father to come and talk to him. The hardest thing I had to do was to tell my father, since I rarely got into trouble at school. My father went with me and I was reinstated. Years later when I needed to fill out an application relative to my school behavior I went to him and asked him if I should report that incident. He asked, "Did you learn to accept your responsibility from the punishment?" I answered, "I surely did." He replied, "Forget it." I didn't and I never shall for it taught me to accept my responsibility and to fulfill my obligations.

MR. MCCOLLOUGH

One of the programs in the high school of MY TOWN which attracted a number of students was called Diversified Occupations, which we named "D.O." for short. The object of the program was to acquaint students with various occupations in which they might pursue a career. It worked by having local businesses offer on the job training for the students. Jobs included beautician, surveying, textiles, and many others. The students would be released from school for several hours each day to work on the job. While they were in school they had to take a course in which they filled out workbooks, read texts, and did other exercises related to their particular jobs. Incidentally, one thing which made this program attractive was that the students were paid for the on-the-job training.

The person responsible for the program when I first began in it was Mr. Jack McCollough. Mr. McCollough was a tall man with an athletic build who had been a coach at one time. He was a charming individual, well liked by students. He related well to the business leaders of the community and was able to place a large number of students. Furthermore, he really knew the vocational aspect of education for he left to head a vocational school in Montgomery.

As a junior, I enrolled, along with Donald Warren, in D.O. as a textile trainee. Almost immediately I hit it off with Mr. McCollough. I would arise about five in the morning, catch a ride to the mill and be at work at six. I would work until ten and then go to school. My first class would be D.O., so I would go in and go right to work. I think my willingness to start to work right away impressed Mr. McCollough. At any rate, we became close friends.

This friendship got both of us into trouble. In the spring of the year, Mr. McCollough planned to have a cook-out for members of the D.O. Club. Since I had physical education the last period, he asked me if I would cut class and assist him with preparation. Wanting to impress him, I immediately agreed. He talked with Coach J. E. "Hot" O'Brien who taught the class I would cut and got his okay. I merrily joined Mr. McCollough and we prepared a delightful meal of barbecued chicken, which all of us enjoyed.

The next morning as I walked into D.O. class I knew that something was wrong from the look on Mr. McCollough's face. He told me that Mr. Clyde Pruitt, the principal, wanted to see me. At that moment I realized that

I had not asked anyone to cover my post as traffic director for the buses the afternoon before. Mr. McCollough tried to say that he would make it okay with Mr. Pruitt, but that I still had to go and talk with him. Apparently, Mr. McCollough did not realize how upset Mr. Pruitt was because instead of Mr. McCollough's "fixing it," I was suspended from school until I brought my father to talk with Mr. Pruitt. Despite what I thought was a failure to protect me, I still count dear my friendship with Mr. Jack McCollough.

After Mr. McCollough's departure, Mr. James Herren, Jr., became our D.O. teacher. He proved to be as knowledgeable and as friendly as had his predecessor. He also became a friend.

MR. LITTLE

Mr. Bennie Little taught me shop. For as long a I can remember, he was the shop teacher. Since all of the boys of my generation had to take shop, he taught all of us. I remember him for several reasons.

When the school board had the new gymnasium built in MY TOWN, they had the lower section at the rear built as a shop. This section of the gym was Mr. Little's kingdom, just as the inside of the gym was Coach J.E. "Hot" O'Brien's.

Since each of us had to take a semester of shop, Mr. Little would set forth the projects which we had to do within a six week period. Among the many things which I cannot do, woodworking is one of them. The first six weeks we were supposed to make a door-stop. The first step was to square our board. By the time I got mine square enough to pass Mr. Little's inspection it was about only two thirds the size it was supposed to be. I really messed up when I had to use a coping saw to cut the top of my board into an arch shape. As pitiful as it was I finally produced something that Mr. Little let pass as a door-stop. He decided with my ability, perhaps the best job for me was in the tool room passing out the tools to my classmates. Although we were supposed to be allowed to work in the tool room for only one six week period, Mr. Little took mercy on me and allowed me an extra six weeks, for which I have always been grateful.

Since the shop was Mr. Little's bailiwick, he had to control all of the boys who were in that end of the building. I remember a couple of boys who wore Mr. Little's patience thin; Buddy Youngblood and Royal "Dude" Jarvis had been itching for a fight for the whole school year. Each would see just what the other could do to be aggravating. All of us boys just knew that sooner or later they were going to have a donnybrook. One day while they were in shop, they began spouting off at one another. Mr. Little overheard them. He told them that he would furnish them with a set of boxing gloves and that they could fight it out the next day. All of us looked forward to shop that day. After roll was called, Mr. Little took the boxing gloves and put them on Buddy and Dude. He took the whole class out behind the gym and told the two of them to go at it. For about ten minutes the two boys battered each other with all that they had. Finally, they began to tire and rather than let one hurt the other, Mr. Little stopped the fight. He warned them that if they did not straighten up there would be a repeat performance.

I remember that Mr. Little showed me up one day. As a youngster I went out for the junior varsity football team. Mr. Little was coach. Since we had to go from school to the football stadium to practice, we often walked. One day as I walked near Coach Little, I challenged him to a foot race thinking that an old man could not out run me. He left me as if I were standing still. I never challenged him again.

COACH

When Coach J.E. "Hot" O'Brien came to MY TOWN, no one realized the impact he would make on the town and its youth during the years he served as coach. No one would have predicted that he would forge a record that would make him eligible for anyone's HALL OF FAME, none of his early players realized that he would make them into part of a legend, but he did.

Coach O'Brien, as I called him, came from one of the smaller colleges in Birmingham, where he had been a star athlete and had earned many awards. Often star athletes do not make good coaches, but he had more than just athletic ability. He possessed a brilliant mind, a zest for life, an understanding spirit, and a love for young people. He enjoyed taking young men with average ability and instilling in them the courage to be greater than they thought they could ever be. It was this that made him the beloved person that he was.

In his years as coach in MY TOWN, Coach O'Brien led his football teams to a string of fifty-seven games without a loss. At that time, the feat was a record among the annals of high school football; only later did Massilon, Ohio's teams surpass it. When that event occurred, Coach O'Brien was one of the few in MY TOWN who refused to make excuses. When Sidney Lanier of Montgomery broke his string at fifty-seven, he accepted it as the gracious gentleman he was. Lest you think his life was always easy and that he could walk on water, as some people in MY TOWN thought, I want to share three stories about him.

Coach O'Brien had a wonderful sense of humor which many people never knew. He loved to play practical jokes and he was an amateur ventriloquist. One day, while standing around at Five Points service station, he saw the young Black man who washed cars washing Clinton Mann's hearse. Unable to resist, he told the young man that there was a corpse in the hearse. Of course, the young man doubted the story, but did go to the back door at Coach O'Brien's insistence. At that moment, Coach O'Brien threw his voice so that the sound appeared to be coming from inside. The startled man jumped back and refused to go near the hearse, despite Coach O'Brien's confession of what happened.

When his teams broke the old record, the people of MY TOWN presented him with several gifts, among which was a new car. He was extremely happy. A few years later, when his teams were not winning and people had begun to grumble that perhaps he had coached long enough, I had a chance to talk with him about the fickleness of people. Even though he was hurt, he refused to speak harshly toward the people of MY TOWN.

One of his favorite jobs was to teach an Intermediate Boys Sunday School Class at First Baptist Church. Because the boys admired him, they would refuse to promote from his class. When it appeared the whole promotion system of the Sunday School would be upset, he offered to resign. Finally, the matter was resolved when a couple of boys agreed to go on to the next class.

Coach O'Brien will always live in the hearts and lives of those of us whom he touched while he coached in MY TOWN. The Alabama Hall of Fame finally recognized the value of such a man to the youth of the world.

THE COLONEL

When Band Director Paul Stewart left MY TOWN to become the Head of the Music Department for the Alabama Baptist Convention, many wondered whom the school board would hire to replace him. Those individuals selected a young graduate from the University of Alabama's music and band program. Since he had studied under the University's famous "Colonel" Butler who had created Alabama's "Million Dollar" band, it was quite natural that the new band director be entitled "Colonel" Edwin Watkins.

Colonel Watkins' appearance in MY TOWN changed the face of the band. First, he secured enough money from the school board to buy new uniforms which consisted of pants for both the girls and boys. He also managed to chisel enough money for some badly needed new instruments. If he could not have a "Million Dollar" band, he was determined to make his a "Half-Million Dollar" band, and he did.

When he first met what was to become his band, he made it quite clear that he expected loyalty and hard work from those who wanted to play in his band. Some members decided that the requirements were too demanding and so they handed in their instruments, but those who remained learned to respect, if not love, the Colonel's discipline. Within a short time it became evident that MY TOWN'S band was one of which we could be proud.

As our "Half-Million Dollar" band prepared for the football season, it had to put in many long and gruelling hours of practice. One almost wished that he was on the football team. The practices would often be in the morning before the sun became too hot or late at night under the lights of the football stadium. During a summer's practice members of the band must have marched thousands of miles.

Besides the long and hard practices, Colonel Watkins introduced some major changes in the band. To my knowledge he was the first director in MY TOWN to have a drum major for the band. He selected a high-stepping, outgoing individual who had an unerring sense of music for the task, W. C Bryant who was also a heck of a baseball pitcher for Coach J.E. "Hot" O'Brien's baseball team.

To show off the talent of his band, Colonel Watkins worked up elaborate half-time shows for the football games. These were sights to behold in themselves. One of these taught me that you never play the role of a drunk man by falling backwards while you are completely relaxed. I had a headache for three days afterwards.

Colonel Watkins had an almost endless patience with the members of his band. I only saw him lose his composure on one occasion. He had called a practice one night and his drummer was late. Since I happened to be an extra body there, with the words, "Anybody can beat the drum," he handed me the drumstick.

The band started at his command and I started beating the drum at what I thought was the right beat only to notice that things got silent rather quickly. Colonel Watkins looked at me and said, "That's alright, J.D., we'll wait for our regular drummer." Not just anybody can beat the drum.

PEOPLE

Every town has its outstanding citizens, its ordinary working people, its characters, and it rogues. MY TOWN was no exception since it possessed a number of each group. It was my fortune or misfortune to meet and get to know a person in each classification and I would like to introduce them to you. I remain confident that you can find at least one of these people who will remind you of someone whom you know.

UNCLE ABE

I still carry his pocket watch which has a dent in the back of it. My grandfather, Walter, passed it on to my father, Marvin, who gave it to me. I will pass it on to my son,Timothy, who will give it to his son Michael. How long this gold watch will be passed along the family remains to be seen. Abraham, "Uncle Abe," traded the watch to Cousin Joe Hornsby for one just like it which he had bought. Both men purchased identical watches, but the one each bought would not run for its owner so they traded and the watches worked fine.

Abraham, "Uncle Abe," as he was known in MY TOWN, was my great-grandfather. He stood about five feet,nine inches and weighed over two hundred pounds. By the time I can remember him, he was bald and had a small white mustache.

Born into the family of Cyrus, Junior, in Harris County, Georgia, as a young man he had moved to work as a farm laborer near MY TOWN. He met and married Miss Martha

Powers. They raised a family which included my grandfather, Walter. Martha died before I was born or at least I cannot remember her. By the time I can remember him, he was living with my grandparents.

They lived on Herd Street in one of the mill houses. The front of the house was built up some ten to fifteen feet above ground so that it would level with the back of the house. "Uncle Abe" loved to sit on the front porch of the house and swing in the swing which hung there. He had gotten too old to do much work and his eyesight was rapidly failing.

I was especially fond of him because he named me. When he was told that my parents had had a boy child, he immediately provided me with my name. He also nicknamed me, "Bud Tucker." I do not know the origin of that nickname.

Over the years "Uncle Abe" developed the practice of going to the banister on the front porch and looking up at the sun at noon to check his watch. He would move from the swing to the bannister, reach into his overalls watch pocket, and remove his watch. Holding it close to his eyes because of his failing eyesight, he would check to see if the watch was keeping good time.

One day, while I was still a very young boy and hardly able to remember it, the mill company sent a crew of carpenters to replace the bannister on my grandfather's porch. They took the old one down, but could not put up

61

the new one right away. My grandfather warned "Uncle Abe" about the absence of the bannister. Old habits,however,are hard to break. On that particular day, as noon neared, "Uncle Abe" arose from the swing, moved to where the bannister was supposed to be,and leaned forward to check his watch. He careened head first to the ground below. The fall proved to be too much since he hit head first, so he died shortly from the fall. As they lifted him from the ground they found him holding to his watch which had a dent in its back. I still carry the watch with the dent in the back and memories of a great-grandfather whom I loved.

GRANDPARENTS

Today many children do not get the chance to know and to be close to their grandparents. I was lucky in that my paternal grandparents lived in MY TOWN and for a long time directly behind where we lived, which created a close bond between them and me.

My grandfather worked all of his life from the time he was nine years old until he reached sixty-five and was forced to retire from the cotton mill. As a younger man he worked in the active production of cloth in the mill, but as he grew older the powers that be decided that he should be transferred to lighter duty and he was assigned to work in the "dope stand." Now let me explain what "dope" was in those days. One used the word to refer to a person who had done a rather stupid act or to refer, as in the case above, to a refreshment stand where one could buy sodas, sandwiches, and other items of refreshment. My grandfather was given the job of cleaning up around the "dope stand." Since the mill worked eight hour shifts and had breaks at designated times,my grandfather did not stay at the mill the entire time. He worked a split shift so that he was at home with my grandmother for several hours during the day. This made for a warm and loving relationship as well as letting them engage in one of their favorite past times -- reading the Bible.

After my grandfather returned from his mid-day shift at the mill and when they had eaten, they would go into what was their living room in their four room mill company house. They would draw up their chairs and my grandfather would take the rather large Bible and begin to read. It was always the King James Version of the Bible for he did not believe there was any other version that was true to the Word of God. He lived long enough to see some of the modern translations, but he refused to accept any of them. After many years of this, my grandfather got to where he could quote the Bible by Book, Chapter, and Verse.

Besides the togetherness and love which I felt my grandparents had for each other, I have always been struck by how simple and yet full their lives seemed to be. The room where they sat and did their Bible reading had two pictures of persons. When I mention this to people and ask them to guess who the two people were, I can tell the age of the individuals by the answer they give. If they say, "Jesus and Franklin Delano Roosevelt," I know that they belong to my generation. Other answers place them in a later time. Most Southerners of my grandparents's time loved those two persons with almost equal fervor. Furthermore, my grandparents never seemed to care about travelling anywhere. They seemed content to be in each other's company as though that was all that they wanted out of life. Times and people's needs were simpler then.

AUNT MATT

I knew her only as "Aunt Matt." Her name was Mrs. Mattie Lou Wright and she was my grandfather's sister which made her my great aunt;nevertheless,everyone in the family called her "Aunt Matt."

I never knew Mr. Wright. As long as I can remember Aunt Matt had lived the life of a widow. She had shared rooms with other widows or elderly ladies who had no one to stay with them. For most of my childhood Aunt Matt shared a house with Mrs. Lemma Hendricks. As one might guess, Aunt Matt became set in her ways as she grew older. Two incidents illustrate just how set she was.

Once when my Aunt Sara and her children were visiting my parents, the youngest child, Margaret,began to misbehave. As is the practice of parents, Aunt Sara said, "Margaret,if you don't stop, I am going to spank you." Margaret continued whatever she was doing. Again Aunt Sara warned, but again Margaret did not stop.

This episode was taking place in the presence of Aunt Matt, whose patience with children was not the longest in the world. Finally, after about six or seven warnings with no action to back them up, Aunt Matt could take it no longer. She looked at Margaret and said,in her most caustic voice, "Honey, you just keep right on doing what you want to do; your mother is not going to spank you." Startled by the comment, a red-faced Aunt Sara took the long-threatened action. Margaret got her whipping.

The other incident took place at my parent's home on the occasion of another visit. At that time my family consisted of my mother, my father,my sister, my mother's youngest brother, and her youngest sister.

Following supper one night as Aunt Matt visited, my sister and my aunt began to giggle in almost uncontrollable fashion at any remark that was made. After this had gone on for several minutes, Aunt Matt could stand it no longer. She said, "You girls are going through giggle hollow and you boys are going down fool's hill.

My uncle spoke up and said, "Aunt Matt, what stage are you going through?" Before she could answer,I quipped, "Plumb pitiful." That remark stopped the conversation as far as Aunt Matt was concerned. I am still amazed that my daddy did not take a razor strap to me for that one. If we were taught anything as children,it was to be respectful to our elders. I guess the spontaneity of the remark saved my hide.

NEVER SURRENDER

Hower Comer Ward died last night. He was one of my heroes. Now H.C. had not been a star athlete in his youth, as a matter of fact, he never played organized sports. He was not a movie star, a politician, or a singer. H.C. was just an uncommon man who refused to quit when the deck was stacked against him;that is what made him one of my heroes.

H.C. grew up in the country around MY TOWN. He lived in a shack on whatever farm his daddy could find to rent. He spent much of his time helping the owner of the farm with the field work. He never really got a chance to go to school for any length of time because he had to help in the field, around the house, and with his younger brothers and sister. His schooling was also limited by his daddy's moving the family every couple of years. He may have gotten through the first six grades.

When H.C. was old enough, his daddy made him go to work in the cotton mill in MY TOWN. He worked hard and regular at that job until December, 1941. There was no question as to what H.C. would do after the Japanese bombed Pearl Harbor;he quickly volunteered for the army. As a matter of fact, for the first time in his life he found out that there were other places than the countryside around MY TOWN.

He was like a kid in a candy store as he boarded the bus to go to Montgomery for his induction. He really bubbled over when he was sent to Colorado with all of its mountains and beauty for his basic training. H.C.'s contribution to the Allies' victory in the South Pacific was not great; he did not prove to be a military hero. The stuff that made him a hero did not show in his army career.

Upon his return to MY TOWN, H.C. went back to work in the cotton mill. He tired of that job and decided to take advantage of Uncle Sam's educational program. He learned a trade and became so good at it that he quit his job in the cotton mill. He preferred to be his own boss and to spend as much time outdoors as he could.

Just when H.C.'s life seemed to settle into a common place pattern, that malady which brought out his heroic qualities struck. Since his army days, he had been in and out of veterans' hospitals. Slowly, but surely, he was losing control of his muscles, which had begun with the ever-so-slow loss of the ability to hold things with a steady grip.

It would have been so easy for H.C. to have cursed his luck, but he refused to do that. He continued to work at his trade until his hands would no longer hold the necessary tools. Even then he would direct his wife as she became his hands.

If he could not use his hands to accomplish his trade, he could use them to work at his hobby of gardening. When the pain was so great that you could see it written in his face, he would climb onto his tractor and plow his beloved garden. Even when his illness had forced him to stop driving, he still climbed that tractor. The fruits of his labor fed him and his family as well as several neighbors.

His was a relentless disease. It robbed H.C. of his speech as well as his ability to move. It drove him to the hospital on numerous occasions, but it never broke his spirit. Even when he lost the ability to speak, he still remained unbroken. His last visit to the hospital was like so many others. When he was told that he would be moved from the intensive care unit to a ward, he said, "Then on Monday I will go home and plant my garden."

His spirit was willing, but his heart just gave out and so one of my heroes died last night. He died planning to return to what he loved and without ever acknowledging that his disease had won.

MISS EFFIE AND GEORGE

MY TOWN was filled with many interesting characters which made it special for me. Two of the most interesting were Miss Effie Lilly and George Powers.

Miss Effie, as I always called her, was really a married lady with a family. She was like an extra grandmother to me. She had always been connected with my family as a neighbor and a friend. Miss Effie was a person prone to speak her mind. She was never shy about voicing her opinion about anything and most everything; in other words, she liked to talk.

George Powers came as close to being a laconic person as anyone I have ever known. He was a man of few words and a dry sense of humor. When I first remember him, he and his sister, Miss Lilly, neither of whom was married, lived across the street from my family and a few doors down from Miss Effie. He could no longer work in the mill due to some health problem.

After the untimely death of Miss Lilly, who was killed in a car wreck in the early 1940's, George rented a place wherever he could find someone to rent to him. Being a bachelor and set in his ways as well as having been spoiled by a doting sister, he was not the easiest person to please. Finally, he wound up in a duplex with my mother and father living in the other side, which was to be expected since he was a distant cousin and since my parents have always shown compassion for needy people.

The incident I want to relate about Miss Effie and George occurred after I moved away from MY TOWN, but on an occasion when I returned for a visit. I was visiting with George on his front porch, when Miss Effie came strolling by on her way to visit her son who lived a few houses down the street. Seeing George and me, she just had to stop and get in on the conversation. Since I had not seen her for a long time, I welcomed the chance for a visit and a short chat.

I am not sure how the subject turned to a discussion of death and funerals, but it did. Miss Effie said, "J.D., I think that every person preaches his or her funeral while they are living and that bouquets should be bestowed upon the living and not on their graves. Nevertheless, when I die I want you to say a few words at my funeral."

Before I could answer that I would be honored to do so, George quipped, "J.D., that won't be hard to do, since all you have to say is that we hope that she has gone to where we know she ain't." I don't know who was the most startled, Miss Effie or me. I knew that George had a dry sense of humor, but I had never seen this side of it.

At any rate, it broke up our conversation and sent Miss Effie on her visit to her son's house. I have always considered this to be one of the most classic put-downs I have ever heard. I still do not know if George was serious.

PICKIN' JACK

I can't remember when I first met Pickin' Jack. It seems he was always in MY TOWN, just as the water tanks and the mill whistle. I knew they were there and I expected them to perform their duty.

To look at him might frighten some youngsters, since Pickin' Jack was tall and gaunt with only one eye. Where the other one was supposed to be was a deep socket that was empty. He had lost that eye before anyone had dreamed of developing and putting in a glass one. Even if such an operation had been offered to him, I doubt that Pickin' Jack would have allowed it since he did not care much about looks.

As a kid I often wondered how he lost it, but I never had the courage to ask him. I later found out that he had been helping someone chop up old car bodies for scrap metal and that a piece of steel had flown off and lodged in his eye. With the medical knowledge available in MY TOWN at that time, nothing could be done to save the eye.

It was not that lack of the eye that made Pickin' Jack a local hero; it was his pickin'.

Many a summer evening after supper, the neighborhood kids would gather around on the back porch of Pickin' Jack's house and beg him to play. I am sure that his voice was not that of a trained "hillbilly musician," but to us he sounded as good as Roy Acuff's "The Great Speckled Bird" and we thought that old Roy himself could not have sung it better.

When Pickin' Jack played the "Chattanooga Shoeshine Boy," we could just see that rag popping off some rich man's shoes. Since we lived close enough to Montgomery and knew that the Pan-American Queen travelled through on its way to New Orleans, when the song came out it quickly became one of Pickin' Jack's most requested numbers. Tears came to our eyes as Jack lifted his melodious voice with the words to "That Silver Haired Daddy Of Mine."

One day I visited Pickin' Jack alone and he began playing and singing a new song called, "Your Cheatin' Heart." I asked him where he had heard it. He told me that a young kid named Hank Williams who had a radio show on a Montgomery station had just written it. He said, "J.D., you watch that boy because he's goin' places."

I never thought of Jack as a prophet, but he sure picked that one right. I often wonder if he were in the crowd that gathered in Montgomery's Coliseum to honor Hank Williams after he made it big on the Grand Ole Opry.

Once when I visited with Jack, I noticed a bruise below his good eye. I asked him how he got it. He said that the night before he and some of his friends had been playing at a honky tonk in the next county and that a fight had broken out, as they often did.

Since it was rather dark in the place, he had not seen a fist flying in his direction and had taken a solid lick under his good eye. He smiled and added, "But when I got up, I decked that ole boy with a beer bottle." I figured from that time on that even with one eye Jack could take care of himself.

Since he could not make a living playing, Pickin' Jack began, during World War II, his own business from his home. He sold cokes and candy from his front porch. Obviously, he became even more popular with the kids.

The last I knew of Pickin' Jack, he was still selling cokes and candy and pickin' out tunes for those neighborhood kids who had not converted to Elvis's music. Pickin' Jack is one of the characters who makes MY TOWN so memorable.

JUMBO

One of my closest friends during my final high school days was Charles "Jumbo" Bates. He earned the nickname because of his bulk in relation to the rest of us skinny boys in high school. By the time he reached high school, he already stood over six feet and weighed upwards of two hundred pounds. Despite his size, Jumbo was the most jovial boy in his class. Because of his size, Colonel Edwin Watkins, the band director, drafted him to play the bass drum in the school band.

I first became acquainted with Jumbo when I went to work in the cotton mill on the Diversified Occupation program at the school. Jumbo was a year ahead of me and had been working in the mill for the previous year. Since we worked from six to ten in the morning and since we had to be at school at ten-thirty, we needed a ride from the mill to school. Jumbo had bought a 1948 Chevrolet coupe and he offered to furnish us a ride for a fee. We were happy to help pay for the gas in return for the means of transportation. I remember that old car had one of General Motors most forgettable engineering failures--the vacuum gear shift on the steering wheel. I do not know how many times Jumbo cursed that lousy gear shift system. Those rides from the mill to school created a bond between those of us who rode--Jumbo, Murray Williamson, Donald Warren, and myself. Of all of the group, I became closest to Jumbo because of our schedule in school.

Both of us wound up in Granny Gibson's English class for our senior year, although Jumbo was a year ahead of me in school. I had taken my junior English in summer school and hence I was in Jumbo's class for senior English. I remember three things about that English class. Once while reading a poem, Jumbo mispronounced the word "dewdrops" saying "drewdrops" and from it came a nickname for me. I was kidded for several months about it. I also remember Granny Gibson asking a question on an exam about the word "bologna" which was contained in a poem. I had enough trouble with understanding the poem without all of the foreign words. Now I had eaten enough "baloney" sandwiches in my life to know what they were, but I had never noticed how the word was spelled. I missed the question and Granny Gibson scolded me for not knowing what "bologna" was. It is ironic that today Bologna, Italy is one of my favorite cities. The last event really took place outside the class. Jumbo needed to pass the course to graduate from high school. He was failing the class for the first two six weeks of the last semester. He and I decided his only hope for passing the course was for me to provide him with some tutoring, hence for the last six weeks we spent several nights per week reviewing English. He made it.

FRIENDSHIP

Several weeks ago I read about the impending marriage of an old friend's grandson. Besides making me realize that I am getting older, the article reminded me of my friend whom I have not seen in a long time. Ours was a friendship born of strange circumstances.

Summer school in MY TOWN was looked upon as a place for those who had failed to pursue their academic endeavors in the fall and spring to attend. No kid in his right mind would think of giving up his summer vacation to study in summer school, unless forced to do so by his parents. Nonetheless, one summer I decided to take an American history course to make my fall load less strenuous. It was during that course that I met Charles Hathcock.

Charles Hathcock was older than I. He had left school to join the service at the tailend of World War II. When he returned from service, he went to work in the cotton mill. For some reason, perhaps because he had travelled and had seen what an education could do, he decided to pursue his high school diploma. He worked in the mill on the second shift, so he could take classes in the morning. That summer he enrolled in the American history class that I was taking. Perhaps because he had been to war, he wanted to learn more about his country.

As we went to class and studied, we began to talk about things in general. One of our most pleasant times was the break we would get each morning. At that time, we would go to Five Points Service Station and buy a coke and a package of peanut butter cookies. As we stood and talked we learned a great deal about each other. I found that although he was older than I, we had a lot in common. One thing that we both thought serious was our studies. Charles because he had come to know the value of an education and I because my Mother and Daddy would tan my hide if I did not do my best in school. We also learned that we shared the same attitude about war. Neither one of us had ever heard of the Greek poet, Pindar, but I was to learn later that Charles and I would have agreed with Pindar when he wrote, "War is a pleasing enough thing for those who know nothing of it, but those who have experienced it feel a strange trembling of the heart at its approach." Charles got his belief from first-hand experience, while I probably got mine from my Father who is one of the most peace-loving men I know.

After I left MY TOWN I would occasionally visit with Charles when I would return home. In the past several years, I have lost touch, but it was nice to read about his offspring's impending marriage. Friendship lives long after personal contacts have become infrequent.

A GENTLE HERO

Fate plays funny tricks. It was a sheer stroke of fate that placed three older guys in my physical education class. I am not sure the reason, but I wound up with Dewey Piper, John Piper, and Sidney Thrash in my class. It was through this experience that I got to know "A Gentle Hero"--Dewey Piper.

In MY TOWN, physical education meant playing softball when it was not raining. Each period there would be about three or four fields where the girls and boys would be playing. Everyone took each game seriously.

In my class, since there were three older guys, one team had two while the other only got one. John Piper was tall and skinny as a rail, so whoever selected him let him play first base. Sidney Thrash was rather stockily built, so if he and John wound up on the same team Sid got to catch. Dewey Piper was just a big guy, but he suffered the same fate if chosen by the same team as John. John's long reach just made him a first baseman.

The event which illustrates Dewey's gentle nature was a squabble in which I was involved. Now there was one thing about me when I played softball--I played to win. Furthermore, I had a big mouth and small brain when I got to arguing.

Most of the time there was no referee for these games; we just depended upon each side to be fair. Sometimes this worked, but it led to a lot of cussin' and fussin' at others, which usually had to be stopped by one of the coaches.

One day I was playing on the team opposite John. Now I was a glove man, but a very poor stick man so every time I came through with a hit I was really proud. Anything close and I would argue about it. I hit a ball to shallow left field and took off running. The left fielder threw the ball to John and I tied with the ball, at least I felt that I had.

I immediately disputed John's call of out. I was several years younger and considerably lighter than John, but I lit into him verbally. Things heated up and it looked like my big mouth had invited a visit from John's fist.

At the very moment that it appeared that John might take a swing, Dewey stepped in, grabbed me, and physically slung me around out of John's reach. After seeing that I was safe, he assumed the role of peacemaker. With his calm voice and gentle manner, he ended the feud. John and I shook hands and resumed the game.

Dewey joined the national guard in his high school days, just as many boys in MY TOWN did. Upon finishing high school, he went into service. He had not been in long before the Korean War broke out. He was sent overseas, where I am sure that he proved as good a soldier as he did a peacemaker.

Dewey became one of the earliest casualties of that war. Every time I watch M.A.S.H., I wonder if one of those units might have had a chance to attempt to save the life of my "gentle hero." News of his death brought home to my generation what my parents had experienced in World War II.

When it came time to build a new national guard armory in MY TOWN, some of the officials wisely chose to name it for Dewey Piper. It was a tribute well deserved by "a gentle hero."

THE BULLY

Every town has a bully and MY TOWN was no exception. I am sure that in many neighborhoods of MY TOWN there were other kids who were called bullies. In mine there was one boy who bossed the kids my age around. He was nicknamed "Porgie." His greatest delight in life seemed to be pushing us around to show how tough he really was. He never resorted to the kind of activity you see on television of some bully extorting candy or money from younger kids, but he sure made it known among us that he was the boss. There were many times when I slipped around a corner to keep from crossing his path.

When I was seven years old, I took scarlet fever. In those days, that disease was considered to be highly contagious. Anyone with it had to be quarantined for several weeks. I was shut off from the rest of my family in a room at the back of the house. The only persons allowed in my room were the doctor and my mother. Even they had to wear special clothes which they left at the door and they had to wash their hands in Lysol antiseptic when they left the room.

It was difficult for a seven year old to be shut off from the rest of his family and friends. I suppose the only thing that made it bearable was the fact that I was extremely sick and I got a great deal of attention from my mother which I always relished. Being quarantined for several weeks and being forced to remain in bed took a lot of strength out of me. I never was a robust kid anyway.

Scarlet fever is not supposed to affect your brain, just your physical strength. I am not convinced that it did not affect my brain. Shortly after my quarantine had ended, I went out to play. One of the first persons I encountered was the neighborhood bully. I do not remember exactly what he said to me that made me mad, but before I realized what I was doing I tore into him and blooded his nose. He went running across the street crying. He ran into his house and told his mother what I had done.

I am sure that I would never have had the courage to do what I did except for the fact that the scarlet fever must have left my brain as weak as my body. Nevertheless, I was feeling pretty good when the bully's mother appeared and scolded me for bloodying her son's nose. In Ancient Greece, when a mortal exercised excessive pride and did something reserved for the gods, it was an act of <u>hubris</u>. In the South of my youth, when a kid exercised excessive pride toward an adult that was an act of <u>hubris</u>. Just as <u>hubris</u> brought the wrath of the gods in Ancient Greece, so it brought the wrath of one's parents in the South. Puffed up with pride about what I had just done to her son, I began to sass the bully's mother. I should not have committed that act of <u>hubris</u> for when she told my mother I got one heck of a spanking.

W. C.

If I were in England I would have to be careful about the use of W.C., but in MY TOWN everybody knew they stood for W.C. Bryant. He came to be known for two things in MY TOWN.

Before Colonel Edwin Watkins came to MY TOWN as band director, the band had usually had a bevy of beautiful young girls as majorettes. Soon after his arrival, Colonel Watkins decided that besides the usual group of pretty majorettes he would like to have his "Half Million

Dollar Band" led by a drum major. This would be a first for MY TOWN, so the Colonel had to select his first drum major with a great deal of care.

Watching drum majors on television causes one to think that it is an easy job which almost anyone could perform. In truth, it is a task that requires athletic and musical abilities. Obviously the individual must be able to withstand the rigors of sustained marching, but he must do more. He must be able to march to a cadence while leading those behind him to keep in step to the music. He must also be able to bark his commands with authority as well as to know when to use his whistle in place of a spoken command. Most of all he must be able to step high and bend backward so that his tall hat almost touches the ground as he marches. In other words, he must be a high-stepping showman. When the Colonel had W.C. try for the job, he quickly recognized that here was MY TOWN'S first drum major.

Besides the above qualities of a drum major, in MY TOWN that individual had to have a sense of humor and to be able to take a lot of kidding. W.C. fit the bill perfectly. Most of the boys teased him unmercifully about being a sissy for his role as drum major. He was able to withstand the kidding and became an excellent performer.

While most of us kidded W.C. about his being a drum major, we also envied him his other talent. Besides being a good student, W.C. was an excellent athlete. He did not play football nor basketball, but he was Coach J.E. "Hot" O'Brien's star pitcher on the baseball team. Many is the game in which I have seen that lanky stringbean of a figure uncork a fast ball that the batter only knew had been pitched when it hit the catcher's mitt. W.C. came to be the man on whom the team depended in the big games and he seldom let the team down.

I think more than any boy in MY TOWN, W.C. changed the minds of those who thought that only a sissy marched at the head of a band dressed in a ridiculously tall hat. He made us realize that being a man is doing what one can do to the best of one's ability.

BILLY ALTON

Someone wrote that practice makes perfect. I do not know about practice making perfect, but it sure does make one a professional. There was one young man in MY TOWN who practiced until he became a professional--Billy Alton.

When most young boys were playing games, such as softball, marbles, or any other of numerous outdoor games, Billy Alton was inside practicing on his piano. Most of the boys poked fun at him for not participating with them. All of us wondered how he could sit for hours at that piano and beat away at the keys. What we did not realize was that Billy was perfectly happy doing that.

Although Billy was several years younger than I, he and I became friends through our participation in youth programs at First Baptist Church. Almost from the time he was big enough, Billy began playing for some group or other at First Baptist. When he was old enough, he became the regular pianist and alternate organist for the church. It was a joyous experience to hear him play the old and lovely hymns on either instrument.

Besides playing for the church, Billy participated in the band at school. In the marching band, he played a number of rather difficult instruments. When Colonel Edwin Watkins needed someone to learn a new instrument for the stage band or even for the marching band, he called on Billy who responded with a dedication that could come only from a person totally dedicated to the field of music.

Although Billy spent much time practicing, he still had time for participating in the youth activities at First Baptist Church. What many people did not know was that Billy had a marvelous sense of humor. He could joke with the best and never really became angry if he were the butt of a joke. Although he remained slim for as long as I knew him, Billy always had a good appetite. He and I put away large amounts of ice cream and cake at church socials and youth parties.

An amazing thing about Billy was that he was not just satisfied with playing music written by others; he composed some of his own. I remember sitting in his living room and listening to some of the most beautiful music that I had ever heard. Upon asking who wrote it, he modestly answered that he had.

After I left MY TOWN and Billy completed his high school education, he moved on to college to study music. Years later I learned that he was giving concerts and had hoped to invite him to visit the university where I teach, but before I could ever arrange it I learned of his untimely and tragic death. I felt that I had not only lost a good friend, but that the world had lost a major talent which had not had time to fully develop. It was a great loss.

COURAGE

Courage is something all of us admire, but at times we have difficulty defining what we mean by courage. Most of us recognize it in the actions of soldiers, firemen, policemen, and other persons whose jobs call for it. Courage is not so evident when a person takes a stand to act in a certain manner despite the criticism which is bound to come his way. During my high school days, one young man demonstrated such courage and inspired me to follow suit.

In MY TOWN the boys and girls took the same classes and shared their play periods until they reached junior high school. At that point in their academic journey, school officials decided to split them up for physical activity courses, but left them together for their academic studies. When they reached high school, they were given more choices as to what they would take as far as their classes. Now it became a standing, although unwritten, rule that girls would take home economics, typing, and business courses; while boys would take shop and other courses thought to be more manly. Anyone who dared to challenge this rule could expect to receive a great deal of kidding from the rest of the students. Nevertheless one young man in my junior year decided to take a typing course and run the risk of being ostracized.

As far as I can remember, Donald Mann was the first boy in my class to decide that he wanted to learn to type. A new young beautiful teacher had been hired to teach the typing class and while many of the older boys befriended her, none would dare to enroll in her class. Knowing full well that signing up for typing would cause him to become the butt of many jokes and snide remarks, Donald decided to go ahead and enroll in the class because he wanted to learn to type. To me that demonstrated courage. Now I have never been accused of being courageous, but I thought that if Donald could withstand the pressure, so could I. Looking back I am not sure whether my motives were as certain as Donald's for that typing teacher sure was beautiful. Anyway both of us took the class and withstood the slings and arrows of our male classmates. I must admit that it was a decision which I have never regretted and which has enabled me to earn a living by being able to type. So I owe a debt of gratitude to Donald Mann whom all of the boys thought was a sissy for taking a typing class.

THEY WON'T STING

Commencement played a big role in the lives of students in MY TOWN. We went to school on what educators called the six-six plan, which meant that we had a commencement from the sixth grade and another from the twelfth grade. We eagerly looked forward to the two events.

I do not remember my sixth grade commencement fully, but I do remember having to wear white pants for the occasion. I also remember the preparation that went into that momentous event. It is not that occurrence, however, that sticks in my mind; it is something that happened as we prepared for it.

Howard Fuller had been put in my class in the sixth grade. He was about six feet tall and weighed about 195 pounds. None of us knew how old he was. Someone had decided that Howard should get some schooling. If he were in school today, he would be placed in a special education class with students of his own ability. In those days, however, nothing like that existed; so he became a member of our class.

I am sure that our teacher, whom we called "the young Miss McNair" since she had an older aunt who taught in our school, must have been at a loss as to what to do with Howard. Since he could not read and since it appeared impossible for him to learn to read the books which the rest of us were reading, she let him do the one thing he did well--draw and color.

He could draw as well as anyone I have ever seen. He spent most of his school day drawing and coloring. Miss McNair was also faced with the problem that most of the boys in the class were picking on Howard, who was as gentle as a kitten. Kids can be cruel and it was cruel the way we made Howard the butt of most of our jokes.

On more than one occasion, Miss McNair had to scold us about making fun of him; as sweet as she was, she could deliver a stern and meaningful lecture on kindness.

Unfortunately, to a sixth grader such a lecture lasts about as long as an ice cream cone in the hands of a hungry boy.

As the time drew near for us to prepare for commencement, Miss McNair told us that we would be using our afternoons to practice. Since Howard was not to graduate, he was left in the room with his pictures and colors. Things went well for several afternoons, but on a particularly beautiful spring day something went wrong.

On this particular day, a swarm of bees swarmed in the oak tree which was located in the northeast corner of the schoolyard. This swarm of honeybees must have measured at least four feet in length and there was no telling how many bees were in it. Miss McNair warned us to stay away from that tree and those bees. We were happy to follow her orders for fear of getting stung.

After lunch, all of us, except Howard, marched to the auditorium to practice for our commencement. When practice was over, we returned to our room. Much to our surprise there was no Howard to be found. Immediately, at Miss McNair's orders, we began to look for him.

While we had been in the auditorium practicing, Howard had decided that he wanted those bees. He knew enough to know that they would not sting him, so he went to the tree and cut them down with his pocketknife. He carried the swarm of bees to his bus and sat down still holding them.

When the bus driver returned to his bus, he could not believe his eyes. He went to the principal, Mr. Pruitt, and told him that a student with a swarm of bees was on his bus. After notifying Miss McNair of Howard's whereabouts, Mr. Pruitt tried to get Howard off the bus with the bees.

To get Howard to agree, he had to promise to put the bees in a croaker sack and to take Howard and his bees home in his car. On that beautiful spring afternoon, Howard, our "slow learner," taught us that he knew more about nature than any of us "smart" sixth graders.

JEROME

Almost every student in MY TOWN looked forward to that time in the spring when school would end and he or she could get involved in summer time activities. One ritual of the spring was a trip to Chewacla State Park near Auburn. Each spring several students would go together and rent a couple of cabins for several days. This was an activity usually reserved for juniors and seniors. In time it became a kind of rite of passage from high school.

The summer of my junior year, several boys who were seniors planned a trip to Chewacla. They made arrangements for a cabin for several days. Among the group was Jerome Jackson. He was finishing his high school career and was planning to go to college at Auburn the following fall. He was a jolly young man who kept his fellow students laughing at his witty antics. Most everyone liked Jerome.

The group could hardly wait for the final bell on that last day. As a matter of fact, they had followed the tradition of wearing overalls which were forbidden during the school year and the wearing of them meant suspension, but what did they care if they were suspended on that last day. The bell did not finish its tolling before the group was loaded into their cars and on the road to Auburn.

They arrived and checked into the cabin. As was the custom, they swore that the last one in the water was a rotten egg. Jerome, despite his bulk, was rather agile and had quickly undressed and slipped into his swimming trunks.

Leading the pack, he headed for the lake. Without slowing, off the end of the pier he went head first. Thinking the water to be deeper than it was, Jerome made a deep dive. He hit the bottom of the lake and stuck. As he stayed in that position for several seconds, the others thought he was clowning. They stood laughing at his antics, when suddenly it dawned on them that Jerome was in trouble. Quickly, a couple of boys jumped into the lake, feet first, and pulled Jerome from the water. They immediately began artificial respiration and called an ambulance. Jerome was rushed to the hospital where it was discovered that he had broken his neck, leaving him quadrapalegic, but at least he was alive.

To facilitate the recovery, Jerome's parents had him moved to Birmingham to the Carraway Methodist Rehabilitation Center which was one of the first of its kind in Alabama. A couple of years later when I visited Jerome at the Center, he said, "J.D., don't worry about someone drowning for it was the peaceful feeling. I lay there in the water, listening to my friends laugh at me, unable to tell them I needed help, but a warm feeling came over me as I drifted into a state of unconsciousness." I thought that maybe it was just one who had a narrow escape talking but it did set me to thinking about how foolish it was to dive head first into a body of water. One's first entrance should be to go in feet first, preferably by wading.

The last word I had on Jerome was that he had recovered enough to work from a wheel chair. He was working to assist others who suffered severe losses.

JIM LACY

Among the things I remember about the Company Store in MY TOWN, two stand out. One of these was a big black scale which had a huge dial on its face. The kids of MY TOWN must have weighed themselves a thousand times on those scales, which we considered to be more accurate than those in a doctor's office. The other fixture at the Company Store was Jim Lacy, who shared the same warehouse with those scales.

Jim Lacy, a rather large Black man, worked at the Company Store as a handyman. He was an elderly man when I first came to know him. He always had a smile which showed off his gold tooth and he walked with a shuffle which was caused by some problem with his feet.

Jim would sit in the warehouse sorting vegetables and discussing various subjects with whomever came by to talk with him. It became a practice for us kids to go to the

100

picture show on Saturday afternoon, to go to the Company Drugstore for an ice cream cone after the picture show, and to go to the Company Store and weigh on our way home. Many an afternoon we would find Jim sitting there sorting potatoes or onions. No matter how many questions we might pester him with, he always took time to be courteous with us.

Years later Daddy started to work for the Company Store and I got to know a bit more about Jim Lacy. I found out that he had a large number of kids. As I think back on the wages of the day, I realize that it must have been difficult for him to provide for his children on his salary, but I never heard him complain about his lot in life. Despite the difficulty of providing for that large family, Jim Lacy insisted that his children stay in school and finish high school. He even provided for several of them to go to Tuskegee Institute. He knew the value of an education and tried to instill that fact in his children. I always admired him for that since so many of the Black kids in MY TOWN went to school only as long as the law forced them to attend.

The other characteristic of Jim Lacy which I admire was his willingness to assist those in need. When I went to work at the Company Store, he took me under his wing and aided me in learning the ropes. He was always generous with his time and wisdom.

I never knew what happened to all of his children, but several served in the armed forces. I am sure that if they followed their father's admonition they turned out to be decent citizens. Jim Lacy was a fine human being, who loved his fellow men.

BUD RUSHIN

MY TOWN was a mill town. The company that owned and ran the cotton mills also built,rented,and kept up the houses of MY TOWN. This meant that the workers in the cotton mills, for the most part, had to secure housing from the housing office of the company.

In order to keep the houses in good repair, the company employed a crew of carpenters,electricians, and plumbers. If any problems developed in one's house,that person informed the housing office which passed on the problem to the appropriate crew. As soon as it could,that crew would fix the problem.

To support these crews, the company secured the necessary supplies. To make sure that the carpenters had the lumber which they needed for repairs, the company ran a planner mill on the Friendship road. Here rough lumber was turned into the necessary size and shape to meet the carpenters's needs.

In order to move the lumber from the planner mill to the job site, the company had a crew of men who would use flatbed trucks to transport the boards. The head of this crew was one of the best known Blacks in MY TOWN, Bud Rushin. He took great pride in his trucks which he treated as though they were his personal property. One could see his smile and the pride on his face as he drove around town delivering lumber.

Bud Rushin was a big man, who stood well over six feet and must have weighed over two hundred pounds. He was not a man to cross. His personality was such that almost everyone in MY TOWN respected him. Bud feared no living man; a corpse was another matter.

The story of how Bud was frightened by a corpse was one of the most frequently told, not in Bud's hearing, in MY TOWN. I cannot vouch for its truthfulness, but I never heard Bud deny it. It seems that a friend of Bud's had died. As was the custom, the corpse was embalmed and brought home in a casket where a wake was held for several nights.

103

One night while Bud was visiting, when he left the room in which the casket was located a group of men decided to play a trick on him. They raised the dead man upright, and placed a lit cigar in his mouth.

Naturally, they had disappeared by the time Bud returned to the room. When he walked through the door and saw the dead man sitting upright with a cigar in his mouth,Bud broke and ran home as fast as he could. He would not come out of his house until the next day. He never found out who the pranksters were and it is probably a good thing, for he feared no living man.

MR. RED

I do not know when Mr. and Mrs. Wilbur "Red" Owens came to MY TOWN. It is possible that like my parents they were born there. When I came to know him, Mr. Red lived with his wife and two daughters, Hazel and Josephine, on Barnett Boulevard.

Like the vast majority of people in MY TOWN, Mr. Red had worked in the cotton mill for most of his life. He worked inside the mill until be began to have severe problems with his lungs. The lint and dust became too much for him to handle, so the company moved him over to work in the filtering plant which purified the water for MY TOWN's water system. It was a job which he could do without suffering with his lungs and it was one which he seemed to enjoy.

I came to know Mr. Red through his daughter, Josephine, who was in my class at school. We became friends and when I became a regular attendee at the First Baptist Church we began to associate in socials. On more than one occasion, Mr. Red and Miss Gertie (Mrs. Owens) hosted our group of young people.

At one of these get-togethers I found that Mr. Red and I had something in common. We both like to eat and our special love was homemade ice cream. On this particular night, he and his wife had invited our group over to their house to eat home-made ice cream. Now as usual they had plenty of cake and cookies to go with the ice cream, but Mr. Red and I decided that we would let the others eat the cake and cookies with their ice cream, while we would stick to eating just ice cream. As a matter of fact, we ate an entire freeze of home-made ice cream between us. We were both full and I think somewhat surprised when we realized that we had eaten "the whole thing." From then on we teased each other about our ability to eat home-made ice cream. Even though we had numerous parties after that, we never duplicated that feast.

Another incident dealing with Mr. Red and me concerns a telephone call. After I had moved away from MY TOWN, one Mother's Day I dialed what I thought was my Mother's telephone number. Direct dialing was new in my area and I had not done it before. When the voice on the other line answered, it was not my Mother but Mr. Red. Realizing that I had gotten the wrong number and not knowing that I could call the operator for a refund, I decided to use my three minutes to talk to Mr. Red. It was nice even if it was done by mistake.

I remember Mr. Red for his friendliness and his kindness towards the young people of MY TOWN. While he never sought any major office in the First Baptist church, he was always one of the strongest supporters of the youth program of that church. He was a man who led by example, not words.

GAYNELL ACHIMON

World War II changed the face of MY TOWN. Many of the young men went to war, while the older men and women who remained went to work supporting the war effort with their labor.

In order to meet the needs which arose from this conflict, a chapter of the American Red Cross was established in MY TOWN. The lady who headed it for most of the war was Mrs. Gaynell Achimon. When there was a need to get a letter to a service man or to get money to one to come home in an emergency, Mrs. Achimon was always available to assist and she knew just what to do. Many soldiers were aided by her in a multitude of ways during the upheaval. One heartbreaking aspect of the task was to notify families that their loved ones had been injured or killed in combat. I am sure that Mrs. Achimon's heart broke on several occasions when she had to perform that duty because of her caring nature.

The other role which Mrs. Achimon filled so long and lovingly was that of leader for the young peoples' class of the Training Union of the First Baptist Church. No one ever loved groups of young people more than she did. I suppose that every young person who attended First Baptist Church from several generations before mine to several after it were influenced as much by Mrs. Achimon as they were by the various ministers. She had a way of talking to young people which they could understand. She never talked down to them, but always listened and guided their thoughts the way she thought they should go. She did this in such a loving manner that the young person to whom she was talking did not get offended.

One of Mrs. Achimon's favorite tasks was to assist the young people in the Training Union class as they prepared for Youth Week each year. She would get the group together and she would give them the benefit of her wisdom as to whom she thought should fill what church office. Most of the time she pegged each person correctly. I am sure that those events went as smoothly as they did because of her love, care, and planning with the young people. Surely, First Baptist Church and the people of MY TOWN, especially the young people, lost a dear friend in her death.

MR. WILLIE

Few men have had more of an impact on my life than "Mr. Willie," which was my Dad's nickname for one of MY TOWN'S most outstanding citizens. I do not know when Wilson Jolly came to MY TOWN, but I do know that as long as I can remember he was associated with the grocery section of the Company Store in MY TOWN.

I first got to know him when my Dad quit the cotton mill and began working for the Company Store. Mr. Willie

109

was a big man who stood over six feet tall and had the muscle to match that height. Despite his imposing size, he was one of the most soft-spoken and gentle human beings I have ever known. He was a man of deep faith who gave many hours of service to his church.

I remember him most for his fairness and his leadership qualities. Working for Mr. Willie was enjoyable most of the time. He did not set himself up as a boss who ordered his help to do his bidding. He showed his co-workers how to work by example and then let them do their job without interference. He took great pride in his co-workers, treating them as family. In today's world, such treatment would be scorned by sociologists and liberal thinkers, but those who worked for Mr. Willie thought it was wonderful.

An example of his fairness involved me. In MY TOWN, as in all towns, there is a social structure based upon wealth. In many cases those who have money think they can run over other people. Mr. Willie would never let that happen to one of his co-workers. One day, as I was driving the delivery truck, the lady in the car in front of me moved over in such a manner that I thought she was going to turn left, so I quickly moved to pass on the right. Suddenly she whirled toward me and into a parking place. I sped up to get out of her way. I recognized her as one of the most influential ladies in MY TOWN. When she saw me, she turned red with anger and I knew that she had recognized

110

me and the truck. I realized that she was going to complain to Mr. Willie. I went immediately to him and explained what had happened, expecting to be chewed out, but he told me to forget it and to be more careful the next time. I was pleased that he had sided with me.

When the Company Store closed, I wondered what Mr. Willie would do since he had worked in the grocery business all of his life. I might have known that he would find a grocery store somewhere. He found it in Jordanville and ran it until his untimely death.

In his last years his eyesight began to fail him. When I last saw him, a few months before his death, I walked right up to him and had to speak before he figured out who I was. As soon as he realized it was me, he began a warm and friendly conversation. I walked away from that meeting with the feeling that Mr. Willie was a big man in more than just size.

MR. PETE

The name Cottle was well known in MY TOWN. The family had been living there for several generations. Members of it held key positions in the mill and other businesses in MY TOWN.

One member of the family was Harold B., otherwise known as Pete Cottle. When it came time for an education, Pete went to college and earned a degree in engineering. Everyone assumed that he would return to MY TOWN and go to work in the cotton mill. Instead he moved his family to New York state and took a job with General Electric.

After working there several years, he decided that the East was not for him and his family, so he returned to MY TOWN. Again everyone assumed that he would use his family's connections to go to work in the cotton mill. He crossed them by deciding to open a business of his own.

He rented a small space in the Mount Vernon Theatre building and opened up a little eating place which he called the Snack Shop. By today's health laws, the place could not have even opened since there were no public restrooms in the space.

To cater to Blacks in MY TOWN, he devised a window through which they could be served, since there were laws against their being served in the interior of the building. They even had to sit in the balcony of the theater.

In the Snack Shop, a person could buy freshly made doughnuts, the first in MY TOWN. They were cake doughnuts and sold three for a dime if they were glazed and two for a nickel if they were plain.

Besides the doughnuts, he concocted a delicious hot dog by adding a mixture of sauerkraut and chili with beans to the wiener and bun. This became one of the most famous foods sold in MY TOWN. Besides these specialties, a person could purchase the usual fare, such as ice cream sandwiches and bars, popcorn, candy, and soda pop.

Mr. Pete was able to surround himself with a loyal and dedicated staff. His right-hand man was Andy Black, who could mix and cook doughnuts like no one else. His only problem was he enjoyed his "spirits" and on more than one occasion, Mr. Pete had to let him go, only to rehire him later.

Mrs. Rosa Harrington went to work for Mr. Pete and remained a faithful employee as long as the Snack Shop remained in business. Others came and went, but all felt they had been fairly treated by Mr. Pete.

The Snack Shop became a profitable and thriving business.   For a man who had earned a degree in engineering, Mr. Pete seemed happier in his own business than working for someone else. There is no telling how many hot dogs and doughnuts as well as other items were sold in the time the Snack Shop operated.   Only the premature and untimely death of Mr. Pete brought it to a close. Indeed Mr. Pete Cottle created an institution in MY TOWN.

MR. ROB

Mr. Robert "Rob" Cottle was known to almost everyone in MY TOWN. Most who were acquainted with him liked him. He had a pleasing personality and charming manner which put anyone in his presence at ease.

Mr. Rob came from humble, but fine stock. His parents were honest, hard-working, Christian people who loved their children and tried to instill the fear of God in them. After the death of his father, while he was still a rather young lad, Mr. Rob worked at various jobs to help support his widowed mother and the other children in the family. This taught him to accept responsibility at a very young age. He gladly undertook the duty and even went on to educate himself.

Since family meant so much to him, Mr. Rob married his childhood sweetheart, Miss Lois. It must have been a marriage made in heaven for it lasted sixty-six years until his death. Surely there were moments of disagreements, but there were many more of deep love that bound two hearts together as one.

Mr. Rob entered business for himself. He proved to be a good business man. He prospered, but he did not let his success go to his head. He continued to cherish the values which had meant so much to him as a young lad. He remained faithful to his teaching about Christianity and he took seriously its admonition to "love others as you would have them love you."

Mr. Rob and Miss Lois shared so much of their wealth with so many organizations that it would be impossible to list all of them, even if I knew them. Probably no one knew all of the groups which he and his wife supported. I do know that one of his favorite institutions was the First Baptist Church of MY TOWN.

Two occasions which few people knew about illustrate his willingness to give of his material blessings for the benefit of others. Whenever the church needed new furniture for the pulpit and the budget would not allow it, he quietly saw that new furniture appeared on the platform. When a young man from First Baptist Church volunteered for the foreign mission fields, he and Miss Lois agreed to pick up half of that young man's salary while the Foreign Mission Board took care of the other part.

Mr. Rob will be sorely missed by those who knew him and benefitted from his wisdom as well as his kindness.

Truly he was a man who loved people and wanted to share with them God's blessings. MY TOWN is the poorer for his passing.

HUMPY

Humpy was his name and movie projection was his game. Humpy Woodall had the perfect job as far as the kids in MY TOWN were concerned. What we had to pay to see, he got to see free. It cost us a dime to see a western movie each Saturday and thirty-nine cents to see a show during the week, but Humpy got to see all of them and he got paid to boot.

I never knew why he was called Humpy, unless it was because he lurched as he walked on his one wooden leg. He

117

was a short, wiry man with an ever-ready smile. He loved the doughnuts and coffee from the Snack Shop and he ate his share of the shop's famous hot dogs. Many was the warm summer nights that he would come around to the shop from his projection booth to order a couple of hot dogs for his supper.

While we thought Humpy's job was absolutely perfect, he did not think so. Once when he invited me into the projection booth with him, I came to the conclusion that he was right. The projection booth was located in the balcony of the Mount Vernon Theater. It was a small room with a glass front that faced the screen of the theater. In the room were two large projectors which operated by a glowing hot carbon rod. The heat from that rod which provided the light for the projector caused the room to be hot in even the coldest weather and to be unbearable in the summer. It was little wonder that on those warm summer nights Humpy often showed up in the Snack Shop with only his undershirt on the upper part of his body.

Besides the heat which made Humpy's job difficult, he had to thread the projectors by hand. Since most pictures required three or four reels, he had to thread the first machine and while it was running he had to get the second one ready. When he switched over to the second one, he had to place reel three on the first projector. This became an endless ritual for the several hours that the movie ran each night. Seldom could he even leave the booth because of the possibility of a break in the film. If that happened he had to be there to splice it immediately or the audience would begin howling and catcalling. Humpy did a fine job for as I think back over the times that I attended the theater I cannot recall a time when the movie was interrupted by a break in the film, except for a minute or two.

MR. B. G. STUMBERG

As early as I can remember, Mr. B. G. Stumberg served as the top man at the mill in MY TOWN and was responsible for the day to day operation of the mills. His was a thankless job for which he received little praise when things went well and much criticism when they were not so good.

I always thought that it was a little unfair that Mr. J. E. Harris made his annual visit to MY TOWN around the fourth of July that the whole town and the mill made such a fuss over him. As far as I could see he had very little to do with the actual running of the mills. He certainly caught no criticism for the short work time when the mills had to be closed; that was saved for Mr. Stumberg.

In keeping with his position, Mr. Stumberg lived in a company house on King Street. He had a maid and a gardener to assist him and his wife with the care of the house. With the assistance of these individuals, the house and the grounds were always very neatly done.

Mr. Stumberg appeared to me to be a strong, silent type individual. I never really remember meeting him, but I did form an impression from what I read about him and what I saw from a distance. He struck me as a man of class and on one occasion he showed me just how much class he really had.

When I graduated from high school, it was such a great event in my life that I decided to cash in on it. I calculated the number of all of my relatives and ordered my graduation announcements accordingly. I must have thought I had more relatives and friends than I did, because when I finished sending them to everyone of whom I could think, I still had a number left.

One day, while at work, one of my co-workers said, "Why don't you send an invitation to Mr. Stumberg?" Now common sense would have told me that you just don't do such a thing. Very few people accuse me of having common sense. At any rate, I decided that I had only a stamp to lose. Off went the invitation with very little thought of a gift in return. Little did I count on Mr. Stumberg's class.

One Saturday night, several weeks later, as I was working, Mr. Stumberg's maid came to the window and asked for me. I was shocked when she handed me a neatly wrapped package and said, "This is your graduation gift from Mr. and Mrs. Stumberg." To say that you could have knocked me over with a feather is an understatement.

When I opened the box, I found a beautiful book, LEAVES OF GOLD, which I added to my library and which I have used many times through the years. When I think back on the rashness of my act and the graciousness of Mr. and Mrs. Stumberg, I realize what class is. I owe them a debt for a lesson in class as well as for a beautiful and valuable book which I cherish as much as the lesson.

THE DIRTY DIGGER

Pete Cottle writes a column, "The Dirty Digs," for THE TALLASSEE TRIBUNE. As is pointed out in the masthead, Pete's is a continuation of one started years ago in MY TOWN by W. G. Eubanks. While I read Pete's writing and find myself disagreeing as often as I agree with him, I want to recall some thoughts about the original "Dirty Digger" and his column.

Mr. W.G. Eubanks worked for the Mount Vernon Mill Company in Tallassee as long as I can remember. He knew my great-grandfather, my grandfather, my father, and me. Since he worked in the office, Mr. Eubanks did not have to keep the two to six first shift nor the two to ten second shift nor the ten to six third shift in the mill. He worked from eight to four with plenty of time to move about town.

Mr. Grover Eubanks became involved in almost every aspect of life in MY TOWN. He served on the board of education for as long as I can remember. He was active in the First Baptist Church, serving as deacon and in several other offices. Any time a need arose for someone to organize a community function, Mr. Eubanks stood ready to assist in any way that he could.

At some point in time, he convinced the editor of THE TALLASSEE TRIBUNE to allow him to write a column about the people of the town. He called his column, "Dirty Digs." In his writings, Mr. Eubanks would relate stories which he had picked up from various individuals. These stories were often amusing incidents that had happened to the person and had been passed on to Mr. Eubanks. Many times he gathered his stories by hanging around the post office where many of the older people would gather to wait until the mail had been placed in their boxes. Naturally as they sat around on the benches, they would trade tales about each other. As a kid, I remember my grandfather waiting until Wednesday afternoon for the paper to come out so he could see if there was a story about him in "Dirty Digs." The column remained a personal column that dealt with individuals. I never remember Mr. Eubanks getting into a discussion of national or international matters in the column. If he did, it was only infrequently. The thing that made the column so popular was the fact that people tended to gather in groups and talk in a more relaxed manner than they do today. Mr. Eubanks was a master at getting people to relate stories to him.

Even after he left Tallassee, he continued the column he had started in 1929 by getting stories and gossip from the town. The nature of the column changed some, but it still remained gossipy. Finally, his health failed him and he had to give up "Dirty Digs." With his insight and wit, he made many people happy by recounting stories about them in the paper.

MISS BRITCHES

Heads turned when she walked into a room. I have seen dozens of men and women stop what they were doing to look at her. When she would enter the Company Store in MY TOWN, everyone would stare. It was not because she was a beautiful as Linda Carter nor as sexy as Brigette Bardot.

In truth she was not beautiful, but she knew how to dress for her job. Because of her "work outfit," someone dubbed her, "Miss Britches." Truthfully, I only knew her as Mrs. Hudson.

Miss Britches's uniform consisted of a pair of men's overalls cut off at the waist. To the cut-off overalls, she took a blue cotton work-shirt and sewed it to them. For her footwear, she chose a pair of men's brogans. She wore her hair in a ball on top of her head and she held the ball in place with a couple of twenty penny nails. These outfits were always clean, and she was a charming woman.

I first came to know Miss Britches because she shopped at the Company Store. Each payday she would come into the store and she would order groceries for two or three weeks. Every second or third payday, she would order a ton or two of feed for her cattle since she lived on a farm several miles from MY TOWN. After I went to work for the Company Store, I came to dread those visits which meant that I had to deliver that large load of feed.

When I worked in the mill, I learned that Miss Britches had a well deserved reputation as being a master craftsman at her job. She worked in the weave shed. Her job was to work among the weavers and to remove the broken threads from the cloth. She was excellent at spotting the broken threads. When she did she would whip out one of those twenty penny nails which held her hair in a ball and with deft strokes she would remove the broken pieces until the cloth was ready to run again. Every weaver wanted her to work in his section of looms.

After I started delivering her groceries and the feed for her cattle, I came to know a little about her. She was an individual like so many in MY TOWN who had to work in the cotton mills. She lived on a little farm where she cultivated vegetables for her family; she even tried to raise a little cotton in her small fields.

Even so, that did not provide her family with enough on which to live, so she took the job in the weave shed. This job was on the first shift, which meant that she had to arise every morning about four o'clock and prepare her breakfast in order to catch a ride and be at work at six o'clock.

She would work diligently until two o'clock when she would catch her ride home. If the weather permitted, she would work her fields until dark. No matter the weather, she always had to milk her cows and tend to her other animals. Life was not easy, but I never heard her complain.

THE OLD MAN AND THE MILL JUDGE

As a junior and senior in high school, I worked in the cotton mill under the program at school called Diversified Occupations. This meant that I would go to work at six in the morning and work until ten o'clock, after which I would go to school for the remainder of the day.

Under the program I was to learn the various processes by which cotton became cloth. Since this meant that every few weeks I would change from one department to another, I was fortunate to meet and learn from many people. Two people stand out as opposite examples of human personality.

One of these individuals was an old man from Notasulga who worked on the clean-up crew for the spinning room. He was an illiterate person as far as reading and writing goes, but he was a master at dealing with human beings.

As a smart alec high school brat, I thought I knew a lot about life, but this old man, in his quiet and gentle ways, taught me more about life than he was able to teach me about cleaning spinning frames. I learned from him that there is never anyone from whom I could not learn something regardless of their formal education or lack of it. It has been an invaluable lesson.

The other person who appeared to be as arrogant as the old man was humble carried title, the "Mill Judge." A plush job in the mill was to be on the fixer crew which rotated from mill to mill and worked in various departments.

The "Judge" was the leader of that crew and he would "judge" any misdemeanor which might be done by one of his crew. In the case of us young boys, it was usually in the form of a kangaroo trial in which we would receive a whack or two from a strap. One day, Donald Warren and I decided to turn the tables.

I went around for a couple of days making smart remarks about the "Mill Judge." Just as we knew he would, the "Judge" summoned me to his "court" (the restroom) during a break. With great bluster I marched into the restroom and a crowd followed. No one noticed when Donald slipped from the room.

After the charges were brought against me and just as the "Judge" was about to administer my whacks, the door flew open and a white cloud appeared in the room. Someone shouted, "A steam pipe has burst!" Men headed

128

out the door as fast as they could scramble, with the "frightened Judge" leading the pack.

I merely rushed to the sink and placed my head over it because I knew that the "busted steam pipe" was nothing more than foam from one of the fire extinguishers which Donald had discharged. He and I cracked up laughing at the "powerful Judge" who had been the first from the room. He was never quite the same and we boys received a more fair shake from the older men.

TWO CHARACTERS

MY TOWN contained many characters, but two especially stand out in my memory. I suppose the reason is that they were used by others to frighten us as kids.

The female character was dubbed, "THE WITCH." This was a terrible thing to do to the poor old soul, but most people in MY TOWN referred to her by that name. After seeing Gravel Gertie in "Dick Tracy," I am convinced that

Chester Could came to MY TOWN and patterned her after "THE WITCH."

The poor woman dressed in long dresses that were always ragged. She wore long sleeves in her blouses and always wore a hat. Even in the hottest summer months she would be clothed in those long, and what must have been almost unbearable, clothes.

The thing which frightened us about her was that she would walk the streets talking to herself. She constantly mumbled as she passed by. Furthermore, she was always stopping to pick up things in the gutter. She would pick up cigarette butts, rubber bands, old bottles, cigarette packages, and any other discarded item which might catch her fancy.

Her appearance and actions made her the perfect person to scare young kids. As I have grown older, I realize that the poor soul must have been suffering from some mental disorder. I often wonder if anyone ever bothered to try to aid her.

The male character which I remember was also suffering from a mental problem. He was never any real threat to anyone, but again those who like to scare young kids used him for that purpose. This young man loved to go to the movies. In order to keep him as occupied as possible, his folks provided him with the necessary funds to attend regularly.

He had a particular seat in which he liked to sit. If someone else got his seat, he would go to the manager of the theater and demand that the person be moved. Most of the time the manager would go and persuade the offender to change seats. Almost everyone in MY TOWN came to know of this habit and they would make sure that they did not sit in his seat.

Again I wonder if anyone tried to help the young man. The amount of knowledge about mental disorders was not as great in those days as now, but still someone might have gotten through to both characters. I do know that it was cruel to use them to scare young kids.

INSTITUTIONS

Every town has those places that become so much a part of the community that they can be thought of as institutions. While there were many of these in MY TOWN, I will introduce you to only those which held a special meaning to me. While you may not be able to say that your town had an institution exactly like these, certainly there are those from your youth that are similar to these.

THE SWIMMIN' HOLE

Lives there a mother who has not said, "Hang your clothes on the tree but don't go near the water?" Or a kid who has not said, "Yes, mother," only to head for the nearest swimmin' hole to plunge in? This is advice which is not so often given today as it was in MY TOWN.

MY TOWN did not have any public swimming pools during my youth. There was a pool open to the public at the Gauntt place, but it was usually crowded and most of the time we could not afford to pay to swim, especially when there was a swimmin' hole closer by. There were several designated places to swim in the many creeks which flowed around MY TOWN.

Shortly after we moved to the country, neither our neighbors, Earl "Sonny" Butler and his sister, my sister, my uncle, nor I knew how to swim, but at the age of ten, eleven, and twelve, we figured that we were not going to get any

133

younger. We cajoled mother into letting us go down to the Butlers to play. What we "forgot" to tell her was that we were goin go the swimmin' hole to play.   Each one of us sneaked our swim suits out of the house and away we went.

What came to be our swimmin' hole was located several hundred yards behind the Butler home at a place in Tuckabatchee creek where a huge tree had fallen into the creek and dammed it up. The water in the hole was only about as deep as we were tall. This meant that by standing on our tip toes we could wade the hole. In this creek my sister, uncle, and I learned to swim.

Later in the year Mother and Daddy learned that we had been sneaking off and going to the swimmin' hole on our visits to the Butlers. They were unhappy that we had sneaked around, but they showed pleasure that we had managed to learn to swim without drowning.

I recall one other experience at the swimmin' hole. One day, Sonny, my uncle, and I slipped off, without the girls, for a little skinny dipping. As we arrived at the swimmin' hole, an old Black man was fishing. If there was one thing that we respected more than our right to swim, it was the right of another person to fish. Although the creek was the Butler property, we did not challenge the old man's right to fish there. We simply offered to turn and leave, but he urged us to swim. We commented that we would scare the fish away, but he said, "Boys, the more you stir the water, the better the fish will bite." All of us laughed to ourselves, but we sure wanted to swim. Into the hole we plunged and within minutes the old man began pulling in sunfish as fast as he could throw out his line. He was right.

Since my youth, I have swum in many places and many types of pools, but my fondest memories are of the old swimmin' hole in Tuckabatchee creek. I wonder if it is still there.

THE COMPANY STORE

Supermarkets are the rage of the day. In almost any town, a person can enter a supermarket and purchase anything from live lobsters to motor oil. When one gets ready to check out, he or she simply pushes his or her basket into a line where a checker will pass each item over a scanner that will automatically record the item and price on a receipt while adding it to the total bill which is furnished after the last item has been scanned. With such electronic gadgetry, it still amazes me that it takes so long to go to the store today. Enough about today's supermarkets, let me tell you about a time when a person did not even have to go to the store in MY TOWN to get his or her groceries.

While most of the stores offered the same services that the Company Store did, I know more about how the Company Store worked. Many of the people who traded with the Company Store worked for the cotton mill. As a courtesy to them, the management allowed them to run a monthly bill for their groceries. As a result many people would simply order their groceries by telephone; others would stop by the store and order their groceries in person. Since several clerks worked in the grocery department, customers developed a friendship with a particular one. When they would call in an order, they would ask for their favorite clerk. They would tell that clerk exactly what items they needed and he or she would write down the list and then set about to gather the goods. When he or she had gathered them, he or she would place them in a box and put them on the shelf outside for the delivery boy to pick up and deliver on his next trip around town. Because a customer would often say to a clerk, "Give me twenty-five pounds of self-rising flour," the clerk had the freedom to send whatever kind he or she chose.

This practice allowed clerks to introduce customers to new products. It also meant that salesmen from the manufacturers would try to keep in good with the clerks by providing them with little presents from time to time.

Once the order was placed on the delivery shelf, the delivery boy would gather a load of orders and fix himself a route so as not to back track and off he would go. The delivery truck was a half ton pickup which was used without a top on fair days, but on rainy ones there was a covered top which could be added to protect the orders from the rain. The person who made the deliveries knew every one in MY TOWN and where they lived. It was something of a luxury to be able to pick up the telephone and have your orders brought to your kitchen without ever having to leave your house. This kind of service exists in only the smallest of towns in today's America. It has gone the way of the passenger pigeon and the dinosaur, but one still misses it.

THE DRIVE-IN

MY TOWN had a movie house as long as I can remember. As a matter of fact, there were two in MY TOWN proper and one in EAST MY TOWN. The Roxy had been closed long before I could remember, but it sat boarded-up on the corner of Sistrunk and James Streets. One night during my youth, the fire siren sounded and the next morning I found out that it was the Roxy which had burned during the previous night. The movie house which we attended as young children was the Mt. Vernon theatre. It would run movies on Sunday through Wednesday and then would switch with the theatre in EAST MY TOWN. The only difference was that both tended to run cowboy movies on Saturday.

Sometime after World War II, some enterprising people in MY TOWN decided to build a drive-in theatre. They looked around for enough land and they found it

138

several miles out of the road known as the ice plant road. They erected the big silver screen, built the ticket booths, the screen booth, the popcorn stand, and aligned the rows in such a manner that the screen could be seen from the farthest row. At each stop, they placed a microphone which could be hung in the window of the car and the sound which went with the action on the screen could be heard by the individuals in each car.

Now the drive-in changed the movie going habits of the teenagers in MY TOWN. I remember the long lines of cars that stretched for miles the first night that it opened. For several months after the opening, one could expect a line of cars a quarter of a mile long waiting to enter the drive-in.

For teenagers who attended the drive-in, it offered a freedom that the Mt. Vernon or the theatre in EAST MY TOWN did not. One could cajole the family car from his parents, pick up his date, and drive to the theatre for the movie and some privacy. Depending on one's date, he tried to either be seen or else not be seen. One's date also determined how close to the screen the car was parked. The closer to the screen the more light and the more people who passed the car on their way to the popcorn stand. Obviously if one wanted considerable privacy with one's favorite girl, the back rows were those of choice.

The drive-in also provided a means of feeding one's date without having to leave the privacy of one's car. At the popcorn   stand the management sold all types of refreshments. This could lead to some disastrous results. I remember one date on which my girl friend had me buy her a large coke. Somehow in the eating of our snacks, she managed to spill the coke all over the front seat. I had a hard time explaining to my parents the wet spot all over the front seat. Luckily it did not ruin the upholstery.

By the sixties, television had progressed to the point that it removed the need for the drive-ins. A couple could stay at home in a room and watch movies or special television programs without the expense of the drive-in; hence most tried to stay alive by running morally questionable films and when that failed they were abandoned. Another American institution bit the dust!

J.T.'S BARBERSHOP

One of the most frightening experiences of a young male child is his first haircut. I cannot remember my first one, but I remember the fright suffered by my son when he was carted off for his first haircut. I feel sure that there was one less barber in that town after cutting his hair.

Even though I cannot remember my first haircut, I can remember those which came afterwards. MY TOWN had several barbershops, but my parents never sent us to them because a friend, J.T. Jones, cut hair in a room in the bottom of his parents home. I recall that about every two weeks, mother would give my uncle and me the ten cents that it cost for J.T. to cut our hair and off we would go to his shop.

J.T. worked in the cotton mill on the first shift, so he would begin cutting hair on Thursday and Friday afternoons about three o'clock. Since he only charged a dime for a child's haircut and a quarter for an adult's haircut, he stayed plenty busy with those who lived within several blocks of his shop.

Because most of the grown-ups would try to come to J.T.'s shop on Saturday due to their work schedule and the fact that he cut hair all day on Saturdays, we kids would try to make it after school on either Thursday or Friday. Another reason that we would almost refuse to go on Saturday afternoon was the fact that the theatre showed cowboy movies at that time. I remember a few occasions when I slipped up and did not get to J.T.'s on Thursday or Friday afternoon and had to beg mother to let me wait until after the cowboy movie to go to get my haircut, which often meant that I would have to wait for an hour or two and caused me to get home for a late supper.

As far as I know, J.T. never went to barber's school, but that did not matter to his customers. They did not want any fancy styles, they simply wanted their hair cut in such a manner that it would look nice. When various styles, such as crew cuts and other fancy cuts came along, those who wanted them had to go some place other than J.T.'s.

His basic haircut was to shorten one's hair, trim it around the neck, and smooth it down with Brilliantine, a hair dressing. One also got a good dusting of powder around one's neck. The rite of passage to manhood at J.T.'s barbershop was when he lathered your neck and shaved the hair on the back of your neck; you had become a man.

Besides providing the neighborhood with good and cheap haircuts, J.T. provided us kids with some valuable advice. It seemed that he always had time to listen to our problems; he was our Ann Landers and most of his advice was better suited to us than hers. I finally felt the peer pressure to go to the "regular" barbershops, but occasionally I would slip back to J.T.'s.

THE DINKY

The people of MY TOWN called the railroad, "The Bump and Slide Easy." Its real name was the Birmingham and Southeastern railroad and it was what is known today as a local railroad, since it ran only about seven miles from MY TOWN to Milstead.

For many years, the B & SE served as the main means of getting freight into the mills of MY TOWN. Freight trains would be brought to Milstead and there the switch engine of the B & SE would attach itself to the train and bring the cargo to MY TOWN. Besides bringing the freight to the mills, the B & SE would also take train loads of cotton products to Milstead to be shipped by the Southern Railroad to other destinations. Before trucks invaded the freight business, the B & SE was a most profitable line.

Along with its freight engine, the B & SE operated a passenger engine called by the local people, THE DINKY. This little gasoline run, self-contained unit would take passengers from MY TOWN to Milstead where they could catch a Southern Railroad train to other places. As a kid, I relished the opportunity to ride THE DINKY. On one occasion, my parents bought tickets for my sister and me to ride THE DINKY to Milstead and back.

The tracks ran from the depot along the Tallapoosa river for several miles and then swung away from the river through the southern edge of Jordanville and along the countryside crossing the road at several places. Finally, a few miles short of Milstead, the track spanned the Tallapoosa river on a trestle. One of the joys of the train ride was that every time THE DINKY came to a road crossing or to the trestle, the engineer would blow the whistle. When weather conditions were just right, the whistle of THE DINKY could be heard in MY TOWN as it crossed the Tallapoosa river trestle. Although the number of riders on THE DINKY had diminished greatly by the time I was a kid in MY TOWN, I still hold fond memories of that old

144

gasoline engine which hauled passengers to and from MY TOWN.

The last time I can remember the B & SE railroad serving passengers was in the spring of my senior year when President Harry Truman mobilized the National Guard unit of MY TOWN. Since that meant that a large group of young men would be leaving for military service in Korea, the powers that be in MY TOWN decreed that there should be a royal send-off. The band with W. C. Bryant as drum major led a parade of the unit through the center of MY TOWN down to the depot. There a number of passenger cars had been hitched to the engine and the soldiers loaded into them to begin their journey to their destination.

As I travel along the road today and see the old B & SE railroad bed, I lament the passing of that era. I long for the return of the passenger train; even THE DINKY would be a welcome sight.

TUBBY'S

New Year's Eve in MY TOWN meant getting a date with one's best girl and going to Tubby's for a hamburger, French fries, a soda, and dancing. If a little sparking followed, so be it.

I don't remember when Clyde "Tubby" Cadenhead came to MY TOWN and opened the eating place which became the hang-out of my generation. I do remember that he built the new brick one which sat on Highway 14 as the two lane road broadens into four going toward MY TOWN. He designed it to cater to all groups of people in MY TOWN. He had an upstairs meeting room which served as the meeting place for many of the civic clubs and which could be rented by others on special occasions. On the ground level, Tubby had a regular restaurant for walk-in customers. In the basement, he had a jukebox, a series of tables, and a dance floor.   This became the weekend hang-out for the young people of MY TOWN.

Besides the different parts of the building designed for various groups, Tubby provided a service which has gone the way of the passenger train. He served drive-in traffic. When I say that he served it, I mean that literally. On a Friday or Saturday night, a couple would likely be confronted by Tubby who would ask what they wanted. He took the order and returned with the prepared food. In all of the times that I went to Tubby's, I do not remember anyone else waiting on me when I drove in.

New Year's Eve parties never seemed to be planned in my day. A group of us would agree that we were going to get dates and would show up at Tubby's at a designated time. We went to the basement and danced until we got hungry and then we moved to one of the tables to order hamburgers, French fries, and a soda. Several of us would sit around and talk until we finished eating, after which we returned to the dance floor and continued dancing until midnight. At the magic hour, each of us made sure that we were dancing with our date because we did not want some other boy kissing our girl as the New Year began.

When the television series "Happy Days" began, I wondered if the authors had somehow visited MY TOWN and had been to Tubby's because "Arnold's" on the show could have been borrowed directly from Tubby's. As the TV series came and went,   so did Tubby's; nevertheless, it saddens me to drive by and see that old building deteriorating which houses so many fond memories.

ROY'S PLACE

Success breeds imitation. Shortly after Tubby Cadenhead proved that there was money to be made in catering to the young people in MY TOWN, Roy Rigsby remodeled a house down the road and opened up his own place. It was not long before he was cutting into Tubby's business at a pretty good clip.

Roy Rigsby was a tall, lean, and lanky man with a sad looking face. Behind that face was a very sharp mind and in that lanky frame was a caring heart. To have looked at him, one would have thought that Roy Rigsby would have nothing

148

in common with young people, since he looked as if he had always been old.

Unlike Tubby's place, Roy's did not have any place for young people to dance. He did have a juke box which stocked all of the current records. In his place were several booths where young people could come and sit while they ate their food and listened to music.

Since this was the days before microphones, Roy would come to the car and take your order if you did not want to go inside. Usually he worked the outside orders by himself. Despite that fact, Roy Rigsby was never too busy to take time to talk with the young people he served. The conversation ranged from small talk about local sports to serious dialogue about growing up. He was willing to share his wisdom with any young person who would listen.

One of my favorite times was to visit Roy's Place after a drive-in movie. If it were a slow night, I would go in and order a hamburger and milkshake. When Roy brought the food, I would begin a conversation about fishing. If there was one subject which he enjoyed, it was fishing. He would tell tall tales about the one which got away, but he would also offer good advice about where, when, and how to fish. Years later when the patterns of young people changed, Roy converted his eating place into a sports shop which featured fishing equipment. He continued to give advice on fishing.

As I think back on those places and men who ran them, I am grateful for the role they played in the lives of the young people in MY TOWN. The youth of today may have the advantages of a larger variety of fast foods, but they are missing a great deal by not having that personal touch of men like Roy Rigsby and Tubby Cadenhead.

EVENTS

Events occur in every town's history which make an impact on those who observe them. MY TOWN has experienced many such during its history. In this section I relate some of those which I witnessed and some in which I took part. Perhaps these stories will refresh the memory of such events in your town and life.

THE PARADE

On December 10, 1940, MY TOWN hosted a big parade to inaugurate the new bridge which had been built across the Tallapoosa river. For years before the only way to cross the river was the old railroad and car bridge on the level with the mills. As MY TOWN grew traffic became too heavy for the old bridge. Working with the state of Alabama, the fathers of MY TOWN convinced the state to build a beautiful new bridge across the river on the bluffs above the mills. Upon its completion a dedication ceremony was planned.

For over a year committees worked on the program for the inaugural opening of the bridge. Among the many ideas which surfaced was that of a parade to cross the river on the new bridge. Not just any parade, but one that would reflect the history of MY TOWN and at the same time impress those state officials who had contributed to the building of the bridge that MY TOWN was on the move.

The parade committee decided that floats representing each major period in the history of MY TOWN should be included. The committee solicited funds from the businesses in MY TOWN. The mill company contributed a considerable amount. At last enough money was raised to put on the most magnificent parade MY TOWN had ever seen.

The next step was to arrange for participants to man each float. Several committees went to work on getting individuals who would agree to dress in period costumes and ride on a particular float. Besides the band, the dignitaries, and some state officials, the floats were manned by individuals who represented Indians, pioneers, Confederate soldiers, soldiers of World War I, and other historical personages from MY TOWN. Several kids I knew were asked to participate by dressing in appropriate costumes and riding on the floats. Boy, was I ever jealous that I was not asked to participate. With hindsight, I am delighted that I was not, because as a spectator I got to see all of the parade and not just a single float.

MY TOWN produced many more parades in the years I lived in it but there is something special about this first one I can remember. It was the celebration of a special spirit and pride that united MY TOWN--a spirit and pride which lives on today.

153

CHRISTMAS

The atmosphere in MY TOWN changed just after Thanksgiving. Even before the mothers of MY TOWN could get the dishes cleaned from serving the chicken and dressing (most people in MY TOWN had chicken rather than turkey for Thanksgiving dinner), one could notice the change.

The first sign was when the men from the mill would put strings of Christmas lights upon the poles that ran through the main thoroughfare of MY TOWN. On each pole from Five Points through EAST MY TOWN would be strung the most beautiful group of lights. When we saw the truck pulling up to those poles, we knew that Christmas could not be far off.

The second sign was that on the Saturday following Thanksgiving. As we would be returning home from our Saturday afternoon Western movie, we would be met on the street near the Company Drugstore by Santa Claus. Now in MY TOWN there was not a Santa Claus on every corner nor for that matter was he on the corner everyday. In MY TOWN Santa Claus would visit the various sections of the downtown area only on the weekends before Christmas. If you wanted to be sure to see him and tell him what you wanted, you had to plan to be in town on the weekend. One thing about our Santa Claus was that we did not have to figure out which was the real Santa Claus because there was only one. We would memorize the list of toys that we wanted and after the movie we would move through the streets until we found Santa Claus. He would listen patiently as each of us rattled off our list. After asking us if we had been good, he would promise to do his best to bring us what we had asked for. As I got to that age of wanting to believe in Santa Claus and not wanting to believe, someone tried to make me believe that the person filling the role of Santa Claus was Mr. John Wadsworth, but with the smugness that can come only from a confirmed believer I pointed out that Mr. Wadsworth was a skinnyman and that Santa Claus must weigh at least two hundred pounds. (I wanted to believe too strongly to give up.)

More importantly than the above signs was the change in the people of MY TOWN. Suddenly people who had not spoken to you in months would greet you with, "Merry Christmas and A Happy New Year!" Somehow you never thought of that act as being a sham; you accepted it as a heartfelt gesture. One seldom met anyone on any occasion that he or she did not depart with a "Merry Christmas and A Happy New Year." For that short time between Thanksgiving and Christmas Day, all of the people in MY TOWN seemed to be one big happy family. My only regret was that the loving spirit did not continue throughout the entire year.

Since I do not get to visit Tallassee much today, I wonder if that same loving spirit fills the hearts and lives of those who live there? I know that it is one of the things I miss the most about living in a larger town. I have yet to have a stranger say to me, "Merry Christmas and A Happy New Year." Even the clerks in the stores seem to have forgotten the Christmas spirit. How sad!

FIRST GRADE CHRISTMAS

Christmas excites kids like no other holiday. One of my most memorable Christmases was the one which I celebrated when I was in the first grade. It was special because of the Christmas party which our teacher arranged for our class. I never did know how she did it, but she convinced the richest man in town to provide her class with a party.

About a month or a month and a half before Christmas, we were told to write on a piece of paper the toy which we would most like for Santa Claus to bring us. Most of the boys listed a toy car or truck or toy pistols. I am sure that I asked for a toy car. Most of the girls wanted a doll or a tea set. Our teacher told us that Santa would see that we got the toy which we listed.

Finally, the day came for us to go to the home of the richest man in town. Most of us had passed the house on many occasions, but none of us had ever been in it. The house sat a little piece from the road and was surrounded by a huge hedge. The driveway was circular and made of stone. The building itself was like a storybook house. It was extremely large and to the eyes of a first grader it was a castle.

We were taken to the house by several of the parents who had cars and who were not working. They loaded us into the cars and off we went on a trip that was never to be repeated in our lives. I am sure that those cars resounded with excited chatter as we neared the site of our Christmas party.

We entered the foyer, left our coats and caps, and then moved into the largest room I had ever seen in my young life. In the corner of that huge room stood the grandest Christmas tree that I had ever laid my eyes upon. Beneath that tree lay a stack of toys that would have made the manager of a department store gleam with joy if they had been bought in his store. There were toys for all thirty members of our class plus presents for the mothers who had brought us and for our teacher.

Even knowing that ice cream and cake awaited us, we all clamored for Santa Claus to bring us our gifts. Our teacher informed us that we were to have the party first and then we would receive our presents. We gobbled our ice cream and cake as rapidly as our little mouths could chew. Finishing our food in what must have been record time, we began to shout for Santa Claus.

Our cry was heard and soon the jolly old elf appeared, all dressed in red. He greeted us with his usual "Ho! Ho!" and "Have you been good boys and girls?" A thunderous chorus of "Yesses" answered him. He then proceeded to pass out our toys. We played with them until time to go back to school and then we took them with us.

There was one toy which caught the eyes of all of us boys. One boy had not asked for the traditional car, truck, or pistols, but had asked for a wind-up caterpillar which had rubber tracks and could climb objects. I do not know where he got the idea for that wonderful toy, but he and it became the envy of all the rest of us boys.

THE WRECK

In the summer of the year after I completed the first grade, something changed in MY TOWN. My parents and the other grownups began to work double shifts in the cotton mills. Strangers began to move into town and housing became extremely scarce. My parents rented a room to a man, his wife, and two young children. He had come to work on the construction of an airport at Tuskegee.

One summer afternoon, late in the season, since my mother was working in the mill and since gas was rationed, the lady offered to drive her car and go out into the country to Mr. Ben Moon's to get some fresh vegetables for us to have for meals. Naturally, my sister and I put in to go with the lady. After some begging, we received permission. Besides my sister and me, the lady asked Miss Lilly Powers to go along and hold the lady's young baby. In the front seat, between Miss Lilly and the lady, stood the woman's young son. In the back was my sister, me, and a dishpan for the vegetables.

As we traveled through the center of Tallaweka, we rounded a curve which was rather sharp at the time. The baby was crying and Miss Lilly was trying to quieten it, but was not succeeding. The lady leaned over to assist and the car drifted into the other lane and into the path of an oncoming car. Inevitably, the cars crashed head-on.

The next thing I knew I was in the local hospital with nurses around me. I was given all of the ice cream I could eat. It turned out that I was one of the two lucky ones in the autos. The young boy who was standing between the two women and I were the only two that escaped serious injury. The lady lost several teeth and suffered some broken bones; her baby and Miss Lilly, along with some people in the other car, were killed. My sister suffered a severe gash across the front of her forehead. It took several stitches to close the gash and the doctors had to shave her head to sew up the wound. That fall when my sister had to start school in the first grade, she had hair as short as mine. Some of the more cruel kids teased her about being my brother. She never let it get her down, however.

There was a hillbilly song, "The Wreck on the Highway," which had a line that went, "I heard the crash on the highway, but I didn't hear nobody pray." I think of the one major wreck in which I have been involved when I hear

160

that song. Shortly after the wreck, the couple and their remaining child moved from MY TOWN

FALL FESTIVALS

One of the exciting times of the school year in MY TOWN was the fall festival. Someone had conceived the idea of each homeroom in school putting on a particular event at a festival. The idea was to raise money for the extra things that the room might want which the school system could not afford.

Planning for the big event, which was usually held sometime in the middle of October, began in earnest in early September. Each class was allowed to decide what it would sponsor. In order to keep from duplicating the teachers agreed on what each one would suggest to his or her class. Each student felt that he or she had a part to play in the planning and the execution of the class project.

On the selected cool October evening before the weather had become too cold to be outside, a crowd would begin to gather about dusk to participate in the festival. Several events were very popular at the carnival-like affair. One favorite was the cake walk. The mothers of the students in the sponsoring class had been asked to bake a cake to be sold at the cake walk. A circle with numbered squares was drawn in the pavement of the parking lot behind the school. A number would be placed on the particular cake to be given away at each walk. People would pay a quarter for the privilege to walk in the circle. Music would be played for a certain time and when it stopped whoever was standing on the number which matched the one on that particular cake won it. I am sure that many a husband was ordered by his wife to walk in the cake walk to try to win the cake she had baked, either because it was so good that she wanted it for her family or it was so bad that she did not want others to taste it.

Another favorite game was the fish pond. A wire was strung around an area and a sheet or several sheets were placed so that those persons who were working in the pond could let the fisherman catch a "fish" without being seen. A person would pay for an opportunity to fish. Taking a pole with a line and a pin on it, the fisherman would place it over he sheet. A "fish" would be attached and the fisherman would reel it in. The "fish" would be some toy or other prize.

At the fall festival during my seventh grade year, Miss Ancille Riggs accepted the idea of a raffle for our class. Naturally I volunteered the object to be raffled--one of my Dad's young pigs. I am not too sure that as the affair turned out that Miss Riggs was happy that she agreed, but we did sell more tickets and did raise more money on that project than any other room that year.

The fall festivals provided an opportunity for the students and their parents to share an evening together in a worthy cause. I do not remember what we bought with our "pig money," but I am sure that it was something Miss Riggs considered worthwhile.

GRAND OLE' OPRY

From the time we got a radio at my home one of our favorite   programs was the Grand Ole' Opry which was broadcast over clear   channel station WSM of Nashville, Tennessee. Every Saturday night we would gather to listen to the announcer as he introduced the program. The show originated in the old Rhyman auditorium   which was a converted church.

The stars of the Opry, as we generally called it, were Roy Acuff, Little Jimmy Dickens, Hank Snow, Ernest Tubb, Tex Ritter, Grandpa Jones, Bill Monroe, Patsy Cline, Minnie Pearl, and Hank Williams. There were several others, but these come to mind.   You could hear a pin drop at our house as Roy Acuff began to sing in that wailing voice of his, especially his "Great Speckled Bird." We would sit silently as Ernest Tubb crooned "I'm Walking the Floor Over You." Novelty tunes such as "I'm My Own Grandpa" and "Sleeping

At The Foot of the Bed" brought laughter to each of us. All of us could relate to Little Jimmy Dickens's predicament at having to sleep at the foot of the bed since we had experienced it at one time or another.

Besides performing on the weekly program, many of the stars had road shows. A troupe of performers which would include a headline star, some backup men, and a comedy act would travel from town to town putting on a show under a big tent. Always after the show and sometimes before it a person could purchase records and pictures as well as albums of the musicians. These people built a following through these visits to small and large towns.

Once a troupe which featured Ernest Tubb was to appear in MY TOWN. My sister and I begged my parents to take us. After much pleading on our part, they agreed. We could hardly contain ourselves until the night of the performance. The tent had been put up earlier in the day. Since it was on a part of the school ground, we had seen the men erect it, which only heightened our anticipation.

I do not remember all of the musicians nor the songs that they sang, but I do remember one important lesson that I learned which took effect only later in my life. The comedy act for the troupe was Lonzo and Oscar. This team was a favorite of my sister and me, so when the time came to buy pictures we began cajoling Daddy for money to buy a picture of them. Both of us wanted a picture of those two comedians. Daddy, in his adult manner and wisdom, suggested that one of us buy a picture of Lonzo and Oscar and the other buy a picture of Ernest Tubb. Neither would agree to the suggestion and insisted that we both get a picture of Lonzo and Oscar. Daddy yielded to our childish ways and bought two pictures of the comedians. I do not know what happened to those pictures, but I later came to realize just how childish we had been since we could have had a picture of two acts of the show rather than two pictures of only one. Most of the time it pays to listen to older and wiser heads, but it is a hard lesson for young people to learn.

COTTON PICKIN'

Several years ago one of the country music singers sang a ballad about turning to robbery and murder before he picked cotton. I was not quite that bad, but I could almost say that I never picked cotton.

The one crop which my Daddy swore he would never plant on any land that he owned was cotton. Daddy had seen and had heard enough about how the South had stuck to that one crop even when it devastated the economy of the region. I also suspect that he knew that raising cotton was a year-round job for which he was not apt to get as full cooperation from his kids as with others.

My one and only experience at picking cotton came when I was a freshman in high school. At the time the football team was winning every game that it played. Our neighbor, Webb Butler, had a son playing on the team and attended most of the games, either at home or away. The team was scheduled to play Valley High School in the Valley, about eighty miles away. Mr. Butler decided that he would take a truck-load of kids to the game in the back of his enclosed milk truck. The price of the trip was two dollars per person.

Since the two younger Butler children, Earl "Sonny," and Betty Ann were close friends of my sister and me, they asked us to go. Immediately, Arie and I began pleading with Mother and Daddy to let us go. We finally got permission, but with one major hitch--we had to work to earn the two dollars. "Not to worry," said Sonny, "Daddy will let you pick cotton to pay the two dollars." To my excited ears that sounded like great news since Webb was willing to pay two dollars per hundred pounds picked. Anyone could pick a measly hundred pounds of cotton, I thought.

Every afternoon after school during the week preceding the game, Arie and I went down to the Butler's cotton field. We would pick cotton for a couple of hours each afternoon. It took only one day to realize that I had been wrong about how easy it would be to pick a hundred pounds of cotton. Cotton does not weigh like cotton-seed meal. By Friday, the day of the game, I had picked just short of fifty pounds. Mr. Butler told me that he would allow me to go on the trip and that I could pick the other fifty-two pounds that I owed him on the following Saturday. I quickly agreed.

The trip was fun and the game was exciting, but as I returned to the cotton field the next morning I began to have doubts about the wisdom of my deal. I faithfully picked up that cotton sack determined to pick my fifty-two pounds that day. At the close of the day, I came to the scales confident that I had done it. My eyes popped out of my head and my mouth fell open when the total of all that I had done for the week came to only ninety-eight pounds. I suppose Mr. Butler saw the pleading in my eyes for he forgave me the other two pounds. I have always been grateful for that since I am not sure I could have picked two more pounds. I can say that was the one and only time that I picked cotton.

THE LONG RUN

Almost every young boy in MY TOWN wanted to be a football player. During my youth, Coach J. E. "Hot" O'Brien's football teams were on a world record course of fifty plus games without a loss. Naturally, the football players were the heroes of all the younger kids. It was even said that most fathers placed a football in the hands of their young sons when they brought them home from the hospital.

I remember a number of wonderful games during my school days, but there was one event which I witnessed that I thought was the most spectacular run that I have ever seen. I have observed many wonderful feats in sports since that time, but none has captured my heart like that one. I was in grade school when it occurred.

The team of MY TOWN was playing some opponent which I do not remember. The key halfback was Bobby Holmes. The game was rather tight as I recall. Our team had backed the other team up to their own thirty yard line. After three downs, they failed to make a first down. Their punter went back into punt formation. Bobby Holmes dropped back to receive the kick. The ball was snapped and their kicker got off a solid punt. The ball spiralled and sailed deep into our end zone. Everyone assumed that Bobby Holmes, to whom the ball went, would down the ball and get it on the twenty yard line. Suddenly, the crowd looked up and Holmes, with the other back blocking, came charging out of the end zone; as a matter of fact, from three yards deep within it. As he came out, the other back threw a good block to spring him free and Bobby was able to pick up blocks from his startled linemen. Quickly, Bobby maneuvered his way past the ten, the fifteen, the twenty, the twenty-five, and gained open field as his linemen knocked down the last defender, except the punter. The only person standing between Bobby Holmes and a one hundred and three yard touchdown was the punter. As the young man charged at him, Bobby Holmes gave the young man as beautiful hip fake as any that has ever been thrown. After that Bobby Holmes completed the longest run that I ever witnessed in the football stadium in MY TOWN. I am not sure that Coach O'Brien did not chew Bobby out for his heroics, but to those of us in the stands it was a deed which we will always remember.

Both the coach and his halfback went on to have great careers in athletics. As a matter of fact, Bobby Holmes went to Southern Mississippi University and on one occasion, he almost pulled off more heroics. His Southern Mississippi team was a big underdog against the highly ranked Crimson Tide of the University of Alabama. With Holmes carrying the ball much of the afternoon, his team almost pulled an upset. It was the only time I ever pulled against the Crimson Tide!

INITIATION

I found something in my closet the other day that brought back memories of one of the most frightening nights and of one of the most determined nights of my life. It was my old high school letter jacket which I am sure that I can no longer wear.

Every boy in MY TOWN wanted to earn a letter so that he could be initiated into the "T" club. There were several ways that one could acquire his letter. The most obvious was to participate in some sport, such as football, basketball, or track. One not only had to participate, but to actually play for a certain number of minutes in the games or the races. The other way was to be a cheerleader. Now since I was the ninety-eight pound weakling advertised in the Charles Atlas commercials, I ruled out football after being sacked, without any kidney pads, by two of Coach O'Brien's biggest linemen. Because I had had such a lousy record as a junior varsity player and because I could not hit the side of a barn with a basketball, I threw the towel in on that one. Hoping to make it at track, I went out for Coach John North's track team where I learned that I was the tortoise in the story of the tortoise and the hare, except the hare never quit running; so I gave that up. The only option left was cheerleader and since I had a big and loud mouth, I was elected cheerleader during my junior and senior years.

At the end of my junior year I was eligible for initiation into the "T" club. This was both the highlight of the year, and also the most frightening. It was even worse than Halloween, because the stories which the members of the "T" club told about what they did to the initiates caused one to welcome the thought of witches and goblins. Nonetheless the night came and we were told to be at the gym at the appointed hour. I prevailed upon my parents to let me drive the car to school that night for the initiation. I thought I could sit safely inside the car until time to go into the gym. With my heart in my throat, I got out of the car and started toward the building. No sooner than I had stepped outside the safety of the car, some of the members began chasing me. I was scareder than a jack rabbit with a pack of beagles on his trail. I took off running as hard as I could. By the time I had exhausted myself and the members caught me, I was suffering from severe pain in my right side.

I did not know whether it was appendicitis or not. At any rate Coach O'Brien recognizing my fear and realizing that it might be appendicitis sent me home. I was not initiated that year. I also lost my chance to haze anyone for I had to wait until my senior year to be initiated.

When the time rolled around during my senior year for initiation, I was determined that I would not flinch a muscle during the initiation. Those guys who had been initiated the year before were laying for me. I think I out did myself for I did not show the first sign of pain during any of the physical punishment which I had to endure that night. Those who had called me a coward for my failure the year before complimented me on my bravery. I was happy that night!

THE CARNIVAL

The children of MY TOWN always looked forward to the latter part of May with great anticipation. Not only was school finished for the summer, but about that time each year the telephone poles would begin to sport posters advertising the coming of Lee Amusement Company. Each year for a period of about two weeks at the end of June and the first of July, with the big day being July 4, the carnival would come to MY TOWN.

The mill would close for the first week in July so that parents could have some time with their children and so the kids could bug their parents about going to the carnival. Only those unlucky persons who had to work on the clean-up crews or some special assignment missed the holiday of holidays, July 4th.

If we were lucky, we could get our parents to take us to the ballpark, where the carnival was located, for a couple

174

of evenings before the big day. Times had to be good and there had to be a little extra money for this to happen. Even if we did not get the extra time at the carnival, there was always the Fourth.

Mother would prepare a meal where we could walk back home for lunch or else she would pack a picnic lunch which we would eat at the park. After she finished, (I often wondered how she did it with us kids nagging her to hurry), we would leave for the ballpark about mid-morning. Until about ten or eleven o'clock that night, we were in heaven at the carnival.

Many of the rides were basic rides, such as the ferris wheel, the tilt-a-whirl, the swings, and the merry-go-round. Lee Amusement Company, however, tried to add new rides from time to time. Some of them were those which I would not try because of their speed and height. Besides the rides there were the games, such as toss-the-coins, ball pitch to knock over bottles, and others.

One summer, I got to work in the carnival. I thought I was in hog heaven until I learned the tricks of the trade and the harshness of those late hours.

One incident about the carnival stands out in my mind. One July 4th, the carnival had added a fun house. One feature of that institution was a female manikin over the entrance and wired with a rather boisterous laughter. As we passed near the fun house, the manikin was going full force.

Someone commented to my mother about its laughter. My mother answered, "She is laughing at all of us fools who are paying ten cents for a Coke." That broke up our crowd with as much laughter as the manikin was making. As you can tell that was a long time ago for many of you cannot remember when Cokes were ten cents, much less the five cents we were paying at local stores.

Lee Amusement Company provided the kids of MY TOWN with a holiday in July that was equalled only by Christmas. Again it was an opportunity for all of the family to participate together in a wonderful experience.

HELICOPTER

Alabama politics always affected MY TOWN. Being as close to Montgomery as it was, politicians frequently made several visits to MY TOWN. The people of MY TOWN kept informed about Alabama politics through "Ole Grandma,"--THE MONTGOMERY ADVERTISER.

The earliest political campaign that I can remember was that of James E. "Big Jim" Folsom in 1946. I remember hearing my folks talk about "Big Jim" and his Strawberry Pickers. It seems that on the day he and his band came to

176

MY TOWN, the whole population turned out to hear him. I must confess that many were probably there to hear the Strawberry Pickers; anyway, "Big Jim" carried MY TOWN and went on to his first term as Alabama's governor.

Four years later when Gordon Persons ran for governor, the method of politicking had become more sophisticated. As a junior in high school, I had become mildly interested in the governor's race. Since I was working for four hours per day in the cotton mill, the campaign provided the topic of conversation for many days and months.

As usual there was a terribly crowded field of candidates. If any of them were to have a chance of winning, he had to find some gimmick. In the 1950 campaign, Gordon Persons found not one but two of the hottest gimmicks of the day--television and a helicopter. He became the candidate identified with these two technological tools of campaigning.

During the campaign, the major topic of conversation centered on how handsome Gordon Persons looked. As he appeared on television, all of the men in MY TOWN, and probably in the state of Alabama, came to believe that every woman would vote for him because of his good looks and sex appeal. Little did I know at the time that he and his family were involved in the local television station in Montgomery. His television appeal was effective because of the growing number of households owning television sets.

Today no candidate dares to consider running a campaign without a media consultant to whom he pays a large part of his campaign budget. Politicians have learned the lesson which Gordon Persons used thirty years ago.

Persons's other gimmick attracted considerable attention also. Prior to this campaign, candidates had travelled the state in cars or, perhaps, a bus. This often proved a tiring and slow way to move around the state, since rest was difficult in a car or even on a bus. Using his money and knowledge of modern technology, Gordon Persons rented a helicopter to travel around the state. This means of travel proved much faster, while at the same time it attracted crowds who wanted to see a helicopter.

I remember when Gordon Persons was supposed to come to MY TOWN. On the scheduled day, the crowd began gathering in front of the Company Drugstore. Word had spread throughout MY TOWN that he would land his helicopter in the large backyard of Mr. Ray Carr, across the street from the drugstore. As the crowd stood in anticipation, a sound like egg beaters began to grow in the distance from the direction of the dam. Heads turned as if on ball bearings and the mouths of the crowd dropped open at the approach of the helicopter. Maneuvering the machine deftly to avoid the power lines, the pilot landed it in Mr. Carr's backyard. Persons emerged from the helicopter, addressed the amazed crowd for about fifteen minutes, re-entered the machine, and lifted off to his next stop having tired himself very little. I think that helicopter, plus his good looks, helped to propel Gordon Persons into the governor's office on Goat Hill. Ah! The wonders of politics!

UFOs

The other night I sat watching a television station from Louisville and the announcer began a program about some people in southern Indiana who claimed to have seen some "Unidentified Flying Objects" or UFOs. One lady even told how she had been taken on board and had seen a rather strange child which she felt was hers by some alien. I found it almost incredible that a major television station would air such story. I expect to find them in the sensational rags at the check-out counters of stores, but I was hardly prepared to experience such a story from the TV media.

Nonetheless, the program set me to thinking of the first time that I heard of UFOs. It must have been the spring of 1950 when I was a sophomore in high school. I had just gone to work in the Snack Shop. Since the shop was located in the building of the Mt. Vernon Theater and since it was the closest eating establishment to the theater, we got quite a number of theater-goers hungry for either one of Pete Cottle's famous hot dogs or doughnuts.

Two of our regular customers, who would come in, buy a coke, sit, and talk for hours on end, were Arthur Summers, Jr. and Houston Hurston. Now both of these young men were older than I and both had started to college at Auburn. One night Arthur came in all excited with news about a report that someone had seen a UFO. Being unfamiliar with the term, I inquired as to what a UFO was. Arthur proceeded to give me a lecture on extraterrestrial beings. I listened with absolute amazement wondering how a supposedly educated person could believe in such hogwash, but I remained polite while he continued. When he had finished, I began in my sophomoric way to challenge this college student. Well, the conversation did not go well for me, but I plunged on ahead to point out that absolutely no proof of such creatures existed. Arthur went away, disgusted that I had not accepted his arguments. A few days later, he came into the Snack Shop and handed me a book, saying,

"O.K., Mr. Smart Alec, read this." He turned and left me with a copy of a book written by some members of an Air Force study group. Basically, the conclusions were that there had been some unexplained sightings of objects which the Air Force could not identify. When he returned, I had to admit to Arthur that maybe he had a point, but I still was not fully convinced that UFOs existed. Nevertheless, as I drove the old winding road up the hill toward my home on the Friendship Road, I kept my eyes peeled for some extremely bright object in the sky. I never saw any and I still remain unconvinced today, despite Carl Sagan.

ANIMALS

No child should have to go through life without owning or, at least having played with, a pet. If you have never experienced a loving relationship with an animal, you will not appreciate the following stories. If, however, you have loved a four legged animal, these stories will captivate you. I was fortunate enough to be raised around pets and farm animals during my childhood. I learned a great deal from my four legged friends.

DOGS

Every child should have the opportunity to grow up with a puppy. There is something about being allowed to have and care for a dog that just makes a person the better for having to assume the responsibility. I was lucky in that my parents felt that my sister and I should have a dog to raise and love. As a matter of fact, we had three dogs and several kittens as we grew up.

I remember well the first dog that my parents got for me. I had been across the alley to my grandparents where I spent a lot of time reading comic books and eating soda crackers. I suppose I lost track of time, which was not hard for me to do when I became engrossed in a comic book. Anyway, my Father came into the house with a scowl on his face and stated that I had better get home right away. When my Daddy made that kind of statement, I moved. All of the way home, I visualized the spanking that I was going

182

to get. Much to my surprise, Mother ushered me into the front room where there was the most beautiful dog that I had ever seen. She was a black and tan mix of a sheepdog and she was named Penny. My parents had gotten her from a Mrs. Stokes who lived in Jordanville. For the next several days we tried to keep her at home, but she would run away back to the Stokes's house. Finally, someone told us that if we would cut a bit of hair from her tail and place it under the front step, she would never run away again. Now I did not believe it, but my Daddy had warned that if she ran away again he would not go and get her. I was willing to try anything. I cut the hair and placed it under the step and, by golly, she never ran away again.

My second dog was Dusty, Penny's son by a red Chinese chow. I remember that Penny was due to have puppies in the spring of 1945. The day that Dusty was born was a bitter sweet day, for it was April 14, 1945, and word reached MY TOWN that the only president that I had ever known had died--Franklin Delano Roosevelt. Raising Dusty was one of the most enjoyable experiences of my youth. Shortly after his birth, we moved to our farm west of MY TOWN. I do not know who enjoyed more the freedom the country offered--Dusty or me. We romped up and down through the woods. He was always digging and once he dug into a hole and brought out a mother possum with nine little ones clinging to her back or in her pouch. As he grew older, Dusty began to loose his hearing and finally, after I had left home, he wandered into the road near our home and was killed by a car.

Blackie, Dusty's son, showed more courage than any animal that I have ever seen. About a year or so after we moved to the country, Dusty sired a litter of puppies and one of them was black and tan like Penny. He was quickly named Blackie and became one of my favorites. As he grew older, he followed us everywhere. One day, Daddy came from the edge of the road carrying the crumpled body of Blackie who had gotten in front of a car. Daddy said, "He is severely injured and will probably die." Mother and Daddy made a pallet in the warm sun at the entrance to the garage. They promised us kids that if he made it through the weekend, they would take him to the veterinarians at the animal hospital in Tuskegee. With a courage that surprised everyone, Blackie not only lived through the weekend, but actually showed some improvement. True to their word my parents took him to the vets. We and they knew that they did not have the money to spend on a dog that was likely to die, but they saw our love and his courage. Although his equilibrium was destroyed, he learned to walk with a cocked head and lived for several more years.

My dogs taught me about responsibility, love, caring, and courage. It is little wonder that I think all children should have a dog!

THE THINGS

Until I was about twelve, we lived in MY TOWN. When I was about that age, Daddy decided to purchase a place in the country. Living in town meant that the number of animals to which we were exposed was limited. We knew what chickens, pigs, cats, and dogs were, but beyond that our knowledge of other animals, especially wild ones, was skimpy. Occasionally, Daddy had shown us geese flying north for the summer or south for the winter. We had heard grown-ups talk about quail, squirrels, possums, and other wildlife but we had not been exposed to them. Since there were no picture books for us to see what they looked like, they remained names only to us.

The spring after we moved, Daddy decided to do some "farming." One day while Daddy was plowing in a field across a branch, Dusty, our part Chow dog, began digging like crazy in a hole along the bank of the branch. My sister, my uncle, and I went to see what Dusty was trying to dig out of the hole. As we got close enough to the place to see what he had, Dusty came backing out of the hole with the strangest sight that we had ever seen. In his mouth, Dusty was dragging, by the tail, this furry creature with a long funny nose. That sight was enough to scare the daylights out of three city kids, but as we looked closer we saw nine little balls of fur attached to the outside of the larger one. Two of us stayed to guard Dusty's catch and to keep him from killing it, while the other one ran across the field to fetch Daddy, whom I am sure had visions of our having been attacked by some monster from the way we were carrying on.

Daddy came hurrying back across the field to where the two guards stood holding Dusty at bay and trying to keep his prize from reaching the hole again. When he ran up and saw what Dusty had captured, Daddy broke into laughter. Naturally, we did not think it was so funny because we had no idea of what Dusty had caught. Daddy explained that our dog had drug a mother possum and her children from their home. The big furry thing was the mother and the nine little ones hanging onto her sides and in her pouch were the babies. Thus, we three city kids met our first possums.

SNAKES

Walking in the woods in the spring, summer, and fall afforded me much pleasure. The only thing that made it an unpleasant experience was the presence of a multitude of different types of snake. I suppose that if there is one thing of which I am deathly afraid, it is a snake, any snake. I never bother to wonder whether or not it is poisonous; I just give it as much leeway as it wants. On more than one occasion, I have encountered snakes in the woods around MY TOWN and each time it cost me about ten years growth. (I would probably be a giant if I had not been scared out of all of that growth!)

One of the chores which we kids had to perform in the summer was to go into the woods and pick blackberries. We knew that that task always meant scratched hands. You cannot pick blackberries without the briars scratching your hands. I am so glad that they have developed a thornless blackberry bush. At any rate, one beautiful summer day, mother told us kids that we should go into the woods on the back of our place and pick some berries. After our usual grumbling, which was to no avail, off we set. We found a thicket of briars that held a huge number of bushes. We approached and began to pick. As usual, I tried every ploy of which I could think to keep from having to pick the berries. I told my sister, my uncle, and my aunt, who were with me, that I would go to the other side of the thicket and pick. I went around the thicket, hid, and rested until I heard them approaching. I jumped up and stuck my hand into a bush. Almost as soon as I had poked my hand into the bush, my eyes spotted it. I jerked back my hand, threw my bucket of berries, screamed, and headed through the woods. After running as far as I could, I collapsed on the ground. When my uncle came to see what in the world was wrong with me, I told him that I had stuck my hand on a snake--a great big diamond-back rattler. I said, "That snake must be fifty feet long and two feet around!" He went back to the house and got Daddy who came and shot it with a shotgun. It turned out to be about six feet long and five inches in diameter. I swear when I first saw it, it looked a thousand times bigger.

In the fall of the year my Dad and I liked to wander through the woods just below our barn. One day, as we were walking along and not paying too much attention to where we were stepping, I took a step over an old log. As I cleared the log, I heard my Dad say, "Look out, a snake!" I stopped about fifty feet away, after I had run through a briar patch and scratched myself all up. Daddy took a stick and killed the rattler, but not before it had scared me half to death.

Even today, I give snakes as much room as they like. I have gotten to where I will not run like a mad man if I see one, but I sure as heck will not pick it up!

WHOA!!

Once my Daddy decided to move to a farm west of MY TOWN, he felt the need to get a horse to plow the fields for him. He found a rather young and, to my childlike eyes, beautiful mare. She was to be his work horse, but we kids convinced him that when he was not working her she should be our riding horse.

One Sunday morning, a week or so after Daddy had purchased the mare and brought her to our farm, a neighborhood kid, Benny Ray Hornsby, came to our house. He had his big red stallion saddled with what I thought was the most beautiful saddle that I had ever seen. He said, "J.D., would you like to get your mare and go riding with me?" I ran to Daddy and begged him to let me go riding with Benny Ray. He said, "Son, you do not have a saddle for the mare." I responded, "I will ride her bareback." Now I had seen enough westerns in which Little Beaver rode his pony bareback along side Red Ryder, so that I knew there was nothing to riding without a saddle. After all, it would be my first time to get to ride a real live horse without someone to lead it. Finally, Daddy yielded when he found that we were going to ride to a neighbor's house which sat off the main road and therefore would not be subjected to passing cars.

I ran to the barn, caught the mare, and put the bridle over her head. The bridle, was a working bridle, not a riding bridle; but how was I, a city kid, to know that. Anyway, after I bridled her, I climbed aboard the horse. Benny Ray and I started down the drive to the main road, which we would have to cross to get to the side road that led to the neighbor's house.

Everything went fine, until we reached the main road. At that point the mare decided that she wanted to go back to her previous owner, so off up the main road she went. No one had ever told this city kid that a horse has a mind of its own and that it can get just as homesick as a kid. At any rate, I soon learned that Little Beaver knew more about riding bareback than I did. With the mare galloping at full speed, all I could do was hang on by grabbing her around the neck.

As soon as Benny Ray saw that I was aboard a run-away horse, he turned his stallion and gave hot pursuit. I suppose the stallion did not have the same desire to pursue the mare as the mare did to return to her former home. At any rate, Benny Ray was not catching up very fast. It was obvious that he could not make his horse overtake my mare. He did manage to yell, "J.D., pull the reins and try to make her go in circles." With a strength born of fear, I yanked down on the reins. The mare began to travel in circles and Benny Ray caught up. What I did not realize was the Daddy had come running up the hill after the mare and me. My days of imitating Little Beaver ended for several months.

HORSE SENSE

After my family moved to the country and my Daddy bought a couple of horses, one of my favorite past times was to go horse back riding. My uncle lived with us at the time and frequently we would take the horses and ride them.

Because Daddy had bought the horses to work, my uncle and I had to make sure that Daddy did not plan for us to plow the horses at the time we wanted to go riding. More often than not we would try to convince Daddy that the horses needed riding so that they would get enough exercise. We had much rather exercise them by riding them than by plowing them. Farm work was never the favorite of either my uncle or myself.

The two horses were different. One was an old horse that was as gentle as a lamb; the other was a young horse that had plenty of pep. When it came to plowing them, I always tried to get the older one; but when it came to riding them I picked the younger one. I am afraid that since I was older, I always pulled rank on my uncle.

One beautiful summer day, while we were out of school and Daddy was at work, my uncle and I decided to take the horses and ride through the woods back behind the fields on our place. We went to the barn and put the bridles on the horses. I took the young one and he took the older one. Because they were work horses, Daddy had chosen not to buy saddles for us to ride so we had to ride bareback. At first it had been difficult for us to ride that way, but as time went on we became quite adept at riding bareback.

On this particular day we set off across the fields and into the woods. We rode through the woods for a couple of hours. Since dinner (lunch in today's vocabulary) was approaching, we decided that we had better hurry to return

192

home. Being late for dinner was one thing that we tried not to do. Daddy had cautioned us about racing the horses, but we figured that since we were late we had better make them run. Off we went at full speed. As we raced through the trees, my younger horse ran off and left my uncle's older horse. It must have been about fifty or so yards in front of him when my horse came close enough to a tree that my left knee caught on it. I still do not know how, but I catapulted over the head of my horse and landed under its hooves. It was at that point that I learned what horse sense was. Instead of coming down with its feet in my chest, my horse jumped completely over me. I do not understand how it did it, but it did. My uncle came galloping up and asked if I was hurt. When I recovered, I said that I was not, but he said I looked like a ghost. I must have been frightened more than I realized. I never galloped through the woods again!

INKY

One of the advantages we acquired when we moved to the country west of MY TOWN was that Mother and Daddy allowed us to have kittens and dogs. We already had a part Chinese chow, Dusty, and his son, Blackie, but we soon added some kittens to the household.

I do not remember exactly when, but at some point after we moved to the country one of our cats gave birth to a beautiful kitten. Unfortunately, this kitten had its two front paws deformed. It could not straighten its front legs so that it had to walk on what would be the elbows of a human. At first we thought about destroying it, since we felt it would have a hard time surviving. My sister pleaded to let her have it and Mother and Daddy relented. Arie named the kitten Inky.

Much to the surprise of all of my family, Inky became one of the best mousers we had. It was amazing to watch that little animal with its seemingly insurmountable handicap do what nature had taught it to do. Inky grew and became more dear to all of us, but especially to Arie who loved that kitten more than any other animal on the farm.

One day, after school, my uncle Bobby who lived with us, Arie, and I had finished our chores and were playing ball in the side yard. I stood at the position which we had fixed as home plate. I was waiting for Bobby to pitch me the ball. At that moment, in a fit of playfulness or stupidity I hollered for Bobby to pitch me the ball for I was going to hit it right at Inky. The ball came toward me and I swung the bat. The bat collided with the ball and as if it had been shot out of a cannon it went straight toward Inky. Before the poor kitten knew what hit it, the ball had broken its neck. I had never dreamed that I could come anywhere close to hitting the ball towards Inky, but in a moment of foolishness I had killed my sister's favorite pet. I immediately began to apologize, but Arie would have none of it; it was weeks before she forgave me. I am not sure that she ever fully believed that I did not purposely kill her kitten. I did learn that one must be careful about clowning around for at times it can have serious and tragic consequences.

GAMES

Today's youth need mechanical toys to entertain them. Without television, computer games, or other electronic devices, they seem to be at a loss as to what to do with themselves. In MY TOWN, we had to find other ways to entertain ourselves since none of these instruments were available to us. Besides the games mentioned in the following pages, many of us spent many happy hours reading books. The games described in the next few pages are some of the ones which we played and which kept us out of our parents's hair. Some will be familiar to all of you and some of you will not have heard of some of them, nonetheless they should remind you of games you played as a child.

ANNIE OVER OR HELL OVER?

One thing missing among kids today is the ability to interact as a group. It seems that most of the games created by toy manufacturers today are geared toward that child who wants to be a loner. In my day, there was no such thing as games like kids have today, but we never seemed to want for something to do.

Most of our games consisted of those which came from the imagination and required few props, mainly more kids. It seemed the bigger the group, the more fun the game. One of the tragedies of today is that kids do not have the chance for the interaction which occurred in our games.

One of the favorite games in the summer months in MY TOWN was "Annie Over" as we were taught to call it. Others called it "Hell Over." I think our Baptist background would not let us use the term "Hell" in any shape, form, or fashion.

I really think "Hell Over" was a shortened name for the term "Hello Over," because Southerners are notorious about eliding vowels, hence "Hell Over." By any name, the game was fun and occupied the neighborhood kids and their parents for many hours during the evenings when the weather allowed.

It was played like this. Two teams were chosen in such a manner that there was an equal number on each side. The captains always tried to balance their team with a mixture of those who had sharp eyes, those who had good hands to catch the ball, and those with speed.

Once the teams had been chosen, the game could begin. First a house that had no fence around it had to be selected for the site. The next ingredient was a rubber ball about the size of a grapefruit or a bit larger. The teams would go to opposite sides of the house. One team would take the ball and shout, "Annie over." The strongest person tossed the ball over the house and the other team tried to catch it before it hit the ground. If a team member caught the ball on the fly, then the team split up and ran around both sides of the house.

The idea was to hide the ball from the team who had tossed it and to try to hit at least one of their players with the ball as the chasing team came around the house. If a team member was hit, that person had to join the other team. This continued in alternating turns until all of the players on one team had been captured by the other.

198

This sounds like a simple, straightforward game, but it was not, since it demanded strategy. For example, one did not want to fall into the habit of throwing the ball in the same direction and with the same velocity every time or the opposition would be able to catch it and chase down the tosser's players. A good tosser would throw the ball high and wide on one occasion and soft and rolling off the roof on another.

Another strategy was to change the direction from which members came. Sometimes members would come around the same side of the house and on others they would split to confuse the opponents as to which group had the ball. One never wanted the same person to carry the ball everytime. Indeed, one of the best tactics was for the larger people to have the ball only infrequently, since they would be the ones expected to have it. Games were won and lost on strategy.

Almost any warm night in the spring, summer, and fall would find a game of "Annie Over" being played by the people in MY TOWN. We may not have had all of the money in the world and our parents may not have given us the toys available to kids of today, but they sure knew how to teach us to live and to get along with one another, a part of which was to develop games that we could all play and enjoy.

199

STEALING STICKS

Warm summer evenings brought all of the neighborhood kids to my street where we would play games. These ranged from "Annie Over" to "Kick the Can." One of our favorites was "Stealing Sticks," which is a variation of "Capture the Flag."

Since there were not many cars in MY TOWN and since those that were were limited by rationing of gas and tires, it was easy for us to take over the streets for our games. "Stealing Sticks" required the entire width of the street.

I think one of the reasons I liked this game so much was that our parents would often join with us. Even though they were working in the mills, sometimes pulling two straight eight hour shifts, our parents always tried to find time to spend with us. These summer evening games were precious to both child and parent.

Since "Stealing Sticks" needed little equipment, it was something we could afford. The materials consisted of several sticks, most of the time they were kindling; a piece of chalk; and a group of people. The area was set by drawing two circles several yards back from a center line and then going and drawing two more at the same distance from the center line in the other direction. A short distance from the center line, a line on each side of it would be drawn. Into one circle on each side would be placed the sticks. The other circle served as that side's "Stink Pot" or "Jail." Now two captains would be chosen and they would select teams. They would be careful to pick large and strong people as well as short and fast ones.

Once the stage was set, the game could begin. The two teams took their respective places on each side of the center line. The object was to steal all of the other side's sticks without getting caught doing it. If you got caught crossing the line to steal a stick, you had to go to the "Stink Pot" until someone could slip through to rescue you.

Another way you could get put in the "Stink Pot" was to try your strength with someone on the other side. If you were pulled over the center line, you wound up in the "Stink Pot." The second line was a zone behind which one could not go, so that a person with long arms might reach across the center line and force you to pull with him.

Because of the object of the game, each team needed to have some small fast people and some large ones who could pull the enemy across the line. This meant that the smaller children who would tend to be fast would be able to play.

I think the opportunity for our entire family to get to participate together in these games with our neighbors kept us closer together. While done in fun, these games developed a sense of competitiveness among us. They also taught us fair play.

I am sorry that the youth of today do not have the opportunity to play simple games that include the whole family. I am sure that they would find some of the inexpensive childhood games exciting, for when I tried to teach my own children this game the whole neighborhood wanted in on it. They thoroughly enjoyed the game and it cost me nothing, but gave me great pleasure.

RED ROVER

The kids in my neighborhood always enjoyed games that could be played by large groups, almost all our play consisted of group activities. Marbles, softball, football, tag, stealing the sticks, and others all required a large group of kids. A favorite game was "Red Rover." I am not sure how it got its name,but it was popular.

To play required only a rather large group of kids. No other equipment was necessary which may be why we enjoyed it so much. Ours was a childhood that did not provide us with a large quantity of store-bought toys, so we had to make do with what our imaginations could concoct.

To begin the game, a captain was elected for two sides. The captains would select members for their respective teams. Once all of the players had been chosen, they would form two lines. At this point strategy entered the picture. In most of our games, boys and girls were included.

Since the object of this game required some strength, the captain was careful how he arranged his line. For example, he tried to avoid placing two girls side by side,since it was assumed that their strength was not as great as that of two boys. He, therefore, tried to place a boy-girl combination next to a boy-girl combination or next to two boys. Having aligned his players, the captain of the side to start the game would call out, "Red Rover,Red Rover, send (the name of one of his opponent's players) right over." The named player ran as fast and as hard as he or she could and tried to break through the line of the other team which was holding hands or arms to try to stop that individual from being able to break the line. If the runner broke the line, that person got to choose a member from the team whose line had been broken and take that person back to the other team. If the runner failed to break the line, he or she had to join the team which had held against the onslaught. This continued in alternating turns until one team had only one person left on it. That team lost. The strategy during the game was to call weak runners to charge your line and send your runners against the weakest point in your opponent's line.

It is a wonder that we did not suffer more scrapes and bruises than we did. No one was ever really hurt playing this game and it provided us many hours of fun without any expense.

RUBBER GUNS

One of the most dangerous games we played was to use "rubber guns" in our battles. This was a game which required some special weapons. The guns were not made of rubber, bur rather shot rubber "bullets."

To make a rubber gun required a piece of wood, a clothes pin, and an old inner tube. For the wood, we liked to find an old apple crate and get the end, which was about twenty-four inches in length and about three-quarters to an inch thick, from it. Once we had the wood, we would draw the outline of a gun barrel about three to four inches wide on it. At one end would be a handle which would be the width of our hands. Upon completion of the drawing, we would get our Coping saws and saw out the gun. After we had it cut out, we would take it and cut notches about three or four inches apart all down the barrel. Then we would take a clothes pin and secure it to the handle with rubber bands cut from the inner tube. The gun was now ready for loading. Starting at the end farthest from the handle, a rubber band cut from the inner tube would be placed over each notch. When that had been completed, a longer strip of rubber from the inner tube was stretched from the end of the gun to the clothes pin trigger. One now had a mighty weapon.

Since I grew up during World War II, which caused a great shortage of rubber in MY TOWN, those of us lucky enough to own pre-war inner tubes counted ourselves fortunate. These tubes provided much more flexible rubber for our guns than the tubes made of artificial rubber of the war years.

Once our guns were ready, we usually chose sides and played one team against another, although individuals would sometimes battle each other. We would hunt each other and try to shoot one another with the rubber bands. The first shot came from the trigger because it was the most powerful and had to be discharged before the others could be. Next came the rubber closest to the trigger, since one would want to shoot his opponent at as great distance as he could. When one was hit, he was out of the game until one team won by being the last one to have a man not shot. Those rubber bands could really sting and we were fortunate that no one got shot in the eyes.

For kids who did not have the luxury of store-bought toy pistols or who preferred the real action that a rubber gun could furnish, these toys were cheap and effective. They provided us with hours of entertainment, not to mention a few stings from rubber bands.

MARBLES

While reading a story about Father Flanagan's Boys Town, I came across a reference to the fact that they played marbles at the first home since that was the only sport for which they had enough money to buy the equipment. The remark reminded me of a lost sport which we played as kids in MY TOWN.

Almost every boy and many girls owned marbles which were their prized possessions. These could vary from beautifully colored glass marbles to steel marbles. They came in different sizes also. Some were bigger than the others. Most boys or girls used the bigger ones as "taws" or shooters. The smaller marbles were the ones at which one shot.

A vital piece of equipment was something in which to carry one's marbles. The most prized item was a tobacco sack, which was many young people's first encounter with tobacco. If one could not get a Prince Albert tobacco can in which to carry his marbles, then the next best thing was a tobacco sack. Least desired was a home-made carrying sack.

Bare ground was essential for playing marbles. When two or more individuals decided to play, some basic ground rules had to be set down. First, was the game to be for "keepsies" or "funsies?" This was a major decision since "keepsies" meant that whoever won a marble kept it.

Second was the type enclosure to be used. There were several types which could be used, such as "pee jinks," circles, or squares. A "pee jink" was a fried apple pie shape drawn in the dirt. The other shapes were what their name describes.

After the establishment of these rules, every player put an agreed upon number of marbles in the enclosure. The choice of who was to shoot first was determined by who tossed his "taw" closest to the starting line. Others followed by their nearness to that line. The person shooting kept on until he failed to knock a marble from the enclosure. Then the next person would shoot until he missed.

A good shooter might clean up before the others had a chance to shoot. One must be careful with whom he played or he could lose all of his marbles.

When we tired of playing marbles in the regular way, there was another game which we played. As far as I know it never had a name. It was where you took a spoon or any other object which could be used to dig shallow holes and dug the holes at different spots in the yard.

The object was to take a marble and to beat your opponents at shooting and ringing the holes in sequence. I suppose this was a type of golf before we had ever heard of that term. At any rate, it provided us with hours of fun in the summer and the fall.

Our childhood games were those which took several kids to play and provided us with fellowship and friendship which many youths of today miss. I suppose the shooting of marbles is limited to the national tournaments which are promoted today. Neighborhood kids don't get out and shoot marbles anymore; their dads would tear their hides if they messed up the green lawn to play marbles.

TOPS

Kids who grew up in MY TOWN had to find ways to amuse themselves. Besides games which did not require any physical equipment, such as tag and hide and seek, we also had marbles, skates, baseball, football, and other equipment for games. One of our favorite toys was a top which we could spin.

The tops which we kids used were not the metal, musical-spinning tops which operated by pressing down on a lever in the middle of it. I suppose that might have been the first top to which most of us were introduced, but that is not the type that we learned to love and to use as we got older. Our tops were round spheres of wood with a metal point in the bottom of the orb. Some of the metal points were rounded themselves, while others were sharp on the end. To make the top spin, one wound the string tightly around the top from the small end to the large end. The end of the

210

string would be fitted around the first finger of a person's right hand. Holding the top in the hand between the thumb and the first finger, a person would give a quick flip of his wrist and the top would fly toward the ground in a spinning motion as the string unwound.

We developed a number of games to be played with our tops. The most simple was to see who could spin his top for the longest span of time. For participation in that game, we tried to use our smaller tops with the sharp metal points, since they seemed to spin for the longest time. (We did not know that the small size and the sharp point worked according to the law of physics to keep down the wind drag. We just knew that the smaller tops spun the longest and that we wanted to win.) Another game which we developed was to draw a line and see who could spin his top on or as near as possible to the line for the longest period of time. Again we chose our smaller tops since we were trying for a long period of time. Another game which we created was to draw a circle and spin our tops in it. The object was to see who could get the most tops spinning at the same time within the circle. A person who got three tops going at the same time usually won. A variation of the circle game was to try to knock your opponents' tops from the circle. For this game we used our larger tops with the rounded metal points since they were harder to dislodge.

My arsenal of tops consisted of three. My favorite in the circle fights was a big round brown one with a rounded metal point. I had a smaller green and red one with a sharp point which I used for endurance contests. My favorite was a red and blue one that was between the other two in size. It had a sharp point and was my favorite for just spinning.

The kids in my neighborhood spent many a happy hour with our tops. Today I never see them for sale in the store. I suppose top spinning has become a lost art!

SKATES

As I sat in a store yesterday, the week before Thanksgiving, listening to Christmas music, I thought that Thanksgiving is a holiday that is becoming lost in the merchant's effort to increase their annual sales. It seems that each year the advertisement for Christmas, which is the merchant's biggest season, comes earlier; as a matter of fact, I actually saw Christmas items being placed on a local store's shelves the week before Halloween. At any rate, the music set me thinking about one of the most prized Christmas presents the kids of MY TOWN wanted--roller skates.

Roller skates were magical wheels for us. They meant that we were no longer confined to games where we had to use our feet as our method of mobility. Now the skates that showed up under our Christmas tree were not the type that kids get today. They were not the kind with the built on boot and rubber wheels that can be used on a skating rink floor and are of little use on the pavement. Our skates had much more flexibility. They were metal skates with metal wheels. Most of us got what we called learner skates at about age six to eight. We really looked forward to getting real skates about our ninth or tenth Christmas. These skates could be adjusted to fit someone with a much larger foot. The magic implement which made it possible to adjust the skates was the skate key.

With the key one attached the skates to one's shoes by tightening the claw like catches on the toes. The heel was kept on by a strap. Since the claws tended to bend the soles of the shoes, our parents forbade us to use our skates with our good shoes. All of us cherished an old pair of shoes that we could use to skate.

Once we had our skates, all kinds of new games were opened to us. A favorite was to play tag on skates. One person would be designated "it" and the others would try to out-skate that individual so as not to be tagged. We would have a safe place to which one could skate and not be caught. Another game was to play stick ball on skates. We would have the bases laid out in the street and the game would proceed just like regular baseball. (I often wondered if this is where they got the idea for "Donkey Baseball.")

213

Besides playing games on our skates, we also engaged in other activities on them. Figure skating, either alone or with a partner, occupied much of our time. Another activity was racing on them. Since we lived on John Street where the street runs downhill into Ann Street, we would take broom sticks from our mothers's old worn out brooms and skate as hard as we could down the hill. As we approached the intersection, we would place the broom stick between our legs and sit down on it, using it as a brake. It is a wonder that we did not get run over by a car coming down Ann Street or fail to stop in time to keep from going over the bluff at the end of the street.

Skates were one gift that we could share with our parents. Often we would talk Mother and Daddy into getting out our skates and skating for or with us. I am sure that we tried all types of maneuvers to embarrass the older folks, but we seldom succeeded.

STRING BALL

Today kids think nothing of asking their parents to go out and buy them a baseball glove, bat, and baseball for several dollars. As a matter of fact, most young boys who reach the age of seven or eight are engaged in some kind of organized baseball program. These programs range from Tee Ball for the youngest to American Legion for the older boys. Equipment for these kids costs their parents a considerable amount of money.

In my day, the kids in MY TOWN did not have baseball gloves, unless they were very lucky. We played ball with our bare hands. It is true that the ball with which we played was not the professional baseball which the kids of today use. It was a ball of string. Our parents would bring home spools of thread from the cotton mill and we would make ourselves a ball. In the center we would place a piece of cardboard, unless we were lucky enough to find a rubber ball--like from jacks. Around this center we would begin to wrap the string, trying to keep the ball about the size of a baseball, then we would raid our father's tool box for his black electrical tape which we would use to cover the ball. At last we had a string ball with which we could play. It was not as lively as a baseball nor was it as hard, but it was a heck of a lot cheaper and for us it worked.

After making the string ball, we would find some kid in the neighborhood who had a bat. After convincing that kid to join in a game of string ball, we were ready to play, except for choosing sides. Two persons were chosen captains. They would pick those players which they thought would be the best. Obviously, there had to be some agreement about the weakest players who had to be allowed to play.

In my neighborhood we did not have a ball field. The neighbor's front yards and the street made up our field. Home plate would be in the middle of the street; with first base being the yard of a neighbor on the right; with second base in the middle of the street; and with third base being the yard of a neighbor on the left. Since cars were scarce and gas even scarcer in those days, we did not have to worry about being run over by cars. We seldom had a game interrupted by one. We did not have to worry about breaking windows, since the string ball was not very hard.

Entire families enjoyed playing in a game of string ball. Mother, father, and kids would all play, with many of them being on different sides, which always made the game more fun. Families played together in those days.

WAGON BUILDING

Our parents did not have a lot of money to give us for major toys, such as bicycles and wagons. This led us to be inventive and creative to secure such items, especially wagons. We developed a technique for building wagons which we valued more than store-bought ones.

The first item of business was to secure the necessary parts. Wheels could be gotten from old scooters, wagons, or roller skates. Lumber needed consisted of a two by four at least six feet in length, some one by sixes onto which could

217

be nailed the axles and which could be used for the seat, and a shorter two by four on which the steering column rested. The metal axles came from old and abandoned wagons. Two empty thread spools served as guides for the steering mechanism. A broomstick served as the steering column. Any wheel could serve as the steering wheel, but most of us tried desperately to find an old car steering wheel to give our wagons real class.

Once the needed items were obtained, building began. The first step was to nail the axles to the boards. Next these boards were attached to the front and back of the long two by four which was to serve as the frame of the wagon.

Upon completion of this step, one moved on to nail the seat and board for the steering mechanism to the frame. A vee would be cut in the board so the broomstick would reach the seat at the proper angle. The broomstick would be secured at the front axle and on the upright board which was about one third of the way from the seat by a couple of pieces of leather nailed over it. To the top end of the broomstick was attached the wheel or the car steering wheel which served to steer the wagon.

After this was done, the really mechanical process started. The spools were attached to each side of the frame about halfway between the seat and the front axle. Next rope was nailed to the front axle board which had been attached to the frame in such a manner as to allow it to turn.

From the front axle board the rope would be drawn under the spools and wrapped in reverse directions around the broomstick and nailed to it which allowed the driver to turn the steering wheel in the proper direction. From this point one could decorate his wagon to be as fancy as he liked.

Once we had built our wagon which was our pride and joy, we would seek other kids to race. The street on which I lived in MY TOWN had a hill which was just made for racing. Wagon building and racing occupied many of our summer hours.

POUND PARTIES

I read an article in a school paper where young ladies are getting upset with young men who ask them for a date and then wind up taking them home to watch a movie on cable or on a VCR. The reason given by most of the boys for this kind of action is that they do not have the money for anything else.

I was reminded of my youth and many of my dates. We did not have money either and we certainly did not have cable or VCRs, but our dates were always fun.

One of our favorite ways to beat the problem of little money and yet provide a good time was to throw a "pound party." Literally one was supposed to bring a pound of something to the party,but this came to mean any kind of food. Some brought potato chips, others cookies,and still others cakes.

The host or hostess furnished the drinks, although sometimes this was shared. If there were to be hamburgers or hotdogs,again the host or hostess furnished them unless it was agreed that certain individuals would bring them.

The idea behind this was to get together a rather large group of friends in a social gathering without anyone spending too much money. A person would decide to furnish his or her house for the party, if he or she could convince his or her parents that it would be a good idea and the crowd would behave themselves.

Once permission was obtained,invitations, by word of mouth were issued to those whom the host or hostess wanted to come. In asking the individuals, the host or hostess made sure that each one understood what he or she was expected to bring.   In this manner the person giving the party kept from having too much of any one item and could also control the menu in this manner.

Everyone was responsible for his or her own transportation. This allowed those who wanted to turn the "pound party" into a date to do so. It also allowed those who wanted to come alone and hopefully meet a certain special young person there to achieve that end. Younger members usually acquired rides with those who had cars or who had permission to use their parents's car.

The difference in these "cheap" dates and those of today are that we wanted to have as many of our friends around as possible. Today young people seem to want to be off to themselves. Groups seem to be out of style today and that is why it appears that the poor young men are cheapskates. Maybe young people should learn about "pound parties."

PARLOR GAMES

Why they were called "parlor games" remains a mystery to me. In MY TOWN most homes did not have a formal parlor, especially the mill company houses. Most of them consisted of four rooms, two for bedrooms, one for a kitchen, and one for what today would be called a family room, which was designated as the "parlor."

Since there were not television sets to occupy the young people of MY TOWN, frequently various ones of our group would pitch a party. This meant that the host or hostess would invite a group of young people to his or her house for an evening of refreshments, usually cokes and cookies or cake, and games. The age of the group would range from the pre-teens to the late teens.

Unlike many parties today, our parents were not banished into another room or from the house. They were active participants in the activities of the evening. Most of the preparation of the refreshments fell upon the ever faithful shoulders of "dear old Mom." The daddy would be the leader in many of the parlor games.

The object of these games, or at least many of them, was to embarrass the participants. Now this was not meant to be mean, but to allow the individual to laugh at himself or herself as others laughed with them. No one was exempt from being the butt of the joke involved in the games.

Several of the games were spin-the-bottle, the barnyard, the Chinese prayer, and post office. The Chinese prayer caused the most embarrassment to the individual. Post office was a game in which the boy-girl relationship was emphasized. It was one which the older kids liked for that aspect of it, while the younger ones liked it as a means of embarrassing each other. Two of my favorites were spin-the-bottle and the barnyard.

To start the game, spin-the-bottle, the host or hostess would spin a coke bottle and whoever the bottle pointed to as it stopped spinning began the game. That individual would say that the person at whom the bottle pointed when he or she spun it would have to sing a song or tell a joke or recite a poem or some other thing. When that person had performed, usually rather poorly, he or she got to name what the next person had to do. All of this was in the spirit of fun and most laughed at their inability to be good performers.

The barnyard game required a bit more planning. Two rows of chairs would be placed one in front of the other. Several people would have been chosen by the leader to play the role of barnyard animals. Each one was to rise, imitate the animal which he or she was playing, turn and bow to their chair, and sit down. The individual who played the role of the farmer would call in the individual on whom the joke was to be played. The farmer would say to the inductee that he had a barnyard, but one animal was missing. The person was to observe the action of each animal and imitate it. Each animal went through its paces. The inductee was asked to be a hen. As he or she rose, cackled, and turned to bow to the chair, the person sitting in the row behind that chair had placed an egg in the seat as though the hen had laid it. The hen would be embarrassed and most would laugh at the joke. The person placing the egg had to be alert for some would make a quick bow and almost sit on the egg.

We spent many hours enjoying these silly and funny games. The friendship and togetherness meant a great deal to us.

MAKIN' ICE CREAM

The kids in MY TOWN knew what store bought ice cream was like because almost every Saturday each one was given money for a cone following the picture show. The brands which were available at the company drugstore came nowhere near as many as one can buy at ice cream parlors today. As a matter of fact, most of us went with either vanilla or chocolate with an occasional kid buying strawberry. After I discovered black walnut, I bought only that flavor and it remains my favorite today.

Even the weekly ice cream cone could not lift our spirits to the level of excitement that came from those rare summer Sundays when Mother would fix an early lunch and Daddy would announce that we were going to Uncle Bubba's and Aunt Sara's. We knew that most of the time that meant that we were going to make home-made ice cream. Mother did not have to coax us to finish our dinner, even our vegetables were eaten with speed.

Following lunch, daddy gathered the ice cream freezer, a box or a sack of salt, and a burlap bag, better known to us as a "croaker" sack. Mother busied herself with getting the ingredients for the ice cream. When they had finished, all of us piled into the car, ready to go.

Our first stop, on most trips, was at Ed Jarrell's service station. Ed ran an ice house next to his station. If he had it, we would purchase a fifty pound block of ice. If by chance Ed was out of ice, we clapped with joy for that meant a trip to the ice plant which was several miles east of MY TOWN. This was a trip we did not get to take often so we loved it.

Having secured the ice, we now made for Friendship where Uncle Bubba and Aunt Sara lived. We looked forward to seeing our cousins, but more importantly we looked forward to that home-made ice cream.

As the women readied the ingredients for the ice cream,the men prepared the freezer. It was an old hand crank freezer with a wooden tub. We children were assigned tasks according to our age. The youngest were allowed to just play, but those who were old enough got the "fun" of turning the crank. Those who were not quite old enough to crank had the task of keeping the hole in the side of the wooden tub open. If the water from the melted ice did not drain out of that hole, then the ice cream would be ruined by the salt seeping into it. We considered this a very important task. Those old enough to crank took turns so that no one would be over-worked. I always liked to take mine first, since it was easy to turn at that point.

At last the crank could be turned no more. That was the clue for the women to break out the bowls and spoons. We children gathered around that freezer like a flock of hungry birds around a bird-feeder on a snow covered morning. More than once our mothers had to step in to keep order as we shoved and pushed to be first. Age taught us that the best was the hardest which came from the bottom of the freezer, but wisdom comes slowly.

I don't know which was best, the ice cream itself or the fun which we had in the whole process of making it. It was a social event that promised a sweet reward.

THE MOVIES

As a youngster growing up in MY TOWN, the movies meant one thing--Saturday afternoon westerns. From as long as I can remember, the kids of MY TOWN looked forward to Saturday afternoons with a great deal of anticipation. Those of us whose parents gave us money to go to the movies were in "hog heaven."

A typical Saturday afternoon went like this. Sometime around or shortly before noon, mother would call us in for lunch or dinner as we called it. After we had eaten, preferably a sandwich, we quickly washed and dressed in our school clothes. When we had completed that task, each of us was given a dime for the movie and a nickel for an ice cream cone at the company drugstore following the movie.

Clutching our nickel and dime, we marched the several blocks to the Mount Vernon Theater. Paying our fare, we rushed to find our favorite seats. Many times we chose those closest to the screen. At 1:50 p.m. sharp, the lights would go out and the list of coming attractions would flash onto the screen.

As soon as that list concluded, a cartoon would begin. It was from watching those cartoons that I learned to love the Three Stooges, Donald Duck, Porky Pig, and a host of other cartoon characters.

After the cartoons ended, we settled down for the serial. Many of us had spent the last week trying to figure how our hero who had been left hanging, tied at feet and hands onto a pole, over a pit filled with alligators would escape. After a few seconds of recap, a new episode would engross us for the next several minutes only to end with our hero in as big a predicament as he had been in at the beginning.

Now we had another week to try to figure out how he could be saved and we had another reason to be sure to return the following week. Next came the thing which had brought us to the theater, the western movie.

Each Saturday, a different western hero rode across the silver screen. For us young boys, the more manly the cowboy the better we liked him. Singing cowboys, like Gene Autry and Roy Rogers, did not thrill us as much as Hopalong Cassidy or Bob Steele. We felt the only time a cowboy should sing was to quieten the cows. Finally, as the picture ended, we would traipse from the theater.

We would march down the street to the company drugstore, to order an ice cream cone. Most of the time we stuck to basic flavors like vanilla, chocolate, or strawberry, but when I learned about black walnut it became my favorite. We ate our ice cream cones as we made our way home.

When we got home, we immediately changed clothes, rushed outside and got our stick horses (there is no telling how many chinaberry limbs I rode to pony heaven). We began a recreation of the western movie that we had seen earlier. Night had to drive us inside.

Habit is hard to break and I had seen so many westerns that I assumed when the lights went on the movie was over. Because of that habit, I remember when I went to see "Gone With the Wind," I sat there until the lights came on and then I left. It was the next week before I found out that there was an intermission and that I had missed the last half of the movie. I never did learn who won that war!

PLAYIN' COWBOYS

Toy manufacturers have produced an electronic gun which can be fitted to a television set to allow children to shoot at individuals on the television screen in certain programs. A means of scoring hits has been devised through some computer method. Already psychologists, anti-violence protestors, and toy manufacturers have enjoined the battle of the effect of such toys on the young people of today. I wonder what they would have said about our form of play as we "shot" each other "playin' cowboys."

Almost every Saturday, the kids in my neighborhood were given a dime for the price of the western movie that was playing at the Mt. Vernon theatre in MY TOWN. Most of us were also provided with a nickel for an ice cream cone following the show. As soon as the show ended, we rushed to the drug store, purchased our cone of cream, and went home as quickly as we could, eating the cones as we went.

At home we changed into our everyday clothes or our cowboy outfits if we had one. We were now ready to "play cowboys."

Each of us had at least one "six shooter," which was like those in the movies that never seemed to run out of bullets (who counts?) For our Trigger, Champion, Silver, Topper, or whatever our favorite cowboy's horse's name, we had chinaberry limbs which we had broken off and shaped to our stride. We were ingenious in our development of those "horses." If we wanted a black horse, we just left the bark on the limb; a white horse called for a skinned limb; while a pinto called for a limb to be carved in a circular motion. If lucky we acquired more than one favorite horse. We used shoestrings for halters.

Once we had changed and had our horses "saddled up," we were ready to choose roles to play. Obviously, all of us wanted to be the good guys. After some debating, so that we could play before dark, some of us yielded and became the villains. For the next several hours, until dark, we rode those stick horses, chasing and shooting each other just as we had seen our heroes do on the silver screen. I do not know how many times I played the role of Hopalong Cassidy (William Boyd: not the freckled-faced gimpy-legged character of literature), Bob Steele, Roy Rogers, Gene Autry, the Lone Ranger, Wild Bill Hickcock, Ken Maynard, and others. On occasions, I even became Tonto, Little

Beaver, or some other sidekick. The game continued until mother's call for supper or darkness drove us inside.

When I think back upon those days, I do not see that there really was any harm. The main difference is that we knew that we were PLAYIN' COWBOYS, not living that life. Today the imaginary world has encroached too deeply into the real world so that young people have a difficulty distinguishing the difference, which is the root of their trouble.

LOOK OUT FOR THE FLAGPOLE

MY TOWN was a football town. Coach J.E. "Hot" O'Brien's teams were on their way to setting a record of fifty-seven games without a defeat. Boys dreamed of growing up to play football for Coach O'Brien and girls grew up wanting to be majorettes or cheerleaders. Friday nights when there was a game at home were like a carnival. From noon on the teachers might as well give up trying to teach because our minds focused on the impending game. I suppose that is why on most of those afternoons of the home games we had pep rallies.

Lest you think that football was played only on the Friday nights that the varsity played let me assure you that it was played every day of the week. One of the favorite pleasures of my childhood was the pick-up games of football in which I participated. Any time a group of kids got together, the odds were that someone would suggest a game of football. Now we did not have enough sense to realize that we could seriously injure one another by playing tackle football without proper equipment. All we wanted was a football; we would take care of the rest.

One of our favorite times to play football was about an hour before school each morning. A group of us boys would gather at the school yard about seven o'clock each morning. We chose sides so that each would be about equally divided as far as talent went. Once we had chosen sides, each captain would call out a number between one and ten. One player from each side would have agreed upon the number. The team of the captain who got the closest to the number received the football first.

Each team would line up at the ends of the schoolhouse which ran parallel with Barnett Boulevard, the busiest thoroughfare in MY TOWN. This provided us with a playing field that was several yards wide and even a bit longer. Besides the danger of the ball going into the busy street, there was one other major danger which our field held--the flag pole which stood in the middle of it. In all of the years that I played on that field--from grade school through high school--I can remember only one person who ran into that flag pole. One morning we had started a game and Sonny "Brownie" Ross, who was younger than most of us but who had a bigger brother Bobby playing on his team, went out for a pass. Sonny must have totally forgotten where he was for he turned and headed down the field as hard as he could run. The ball was thrown to him and about the time he caught it and turned he smacked directly into the flag pole at full speed! He was knocked out as cold as a potato. Immediately, someone ran inside and told Mr. Clyde Pruitt, the principal, about the accident. He came out and halted our football games on the front lawn of the schoolhouse. Luckily for Sonny, he only had a mild concussion. From then on no one had to tell Sonny to "look out for the flag pole."

BOMBS AWAY

I write this story under duress. My Daddy and a friend of mine told me that if I did not write this one that my friend would write it and my daddy would have it published under my name. Since I guess confession is good for the soul, here is the story.

I was born and raised in town until the year between my twelfth and thirteenth birthdays. In that year my parents decided that they would move us to a small farm which they had bought in the country about two miles west of MY TOWN. I must confess that my sister, my uncle and aunt who were living with us, and I were not all that enchanted with the idea of moving to the country. We had become accustomed to such luxuries as running water, an indoor toilet, and a coal burning fire-place. We did not like the idea of moving into a house with none of those conveniences

235

except the fireplace. Nonetheless, we moved and, in the course of time, learned to love it.

On our back-porch was our well, which was enclosed and had a windlass. We would let the bucket down into the well and draw fresh water, some of the freshest and best tasting water in the area even better than the water we had had in town.

One day, out of boredom when it was raining and we could not play outside, my uncle and I invented a new game, "Bombs Away!" We discovered that if we let the bucket down about half way toward the bottom of the well, it would make a good target for us to "bomb" with Irish potatoes which Daddy had dug and had placed on the well porch for the winter and for mother to use as she needed them. After all, if we missed the bucket, the potatoes would sink to the bottom of the well, never to be heard from again. Little did we city boys know that while the potatoes would sink immediately they would eventually rot and rise up to the top of the water in the well. We had a ball "bombing" the bucket.

Several weeks later, we overheard Daddy say to Mother that the water in the well surely did stink. A day or so later he drew up a rotten potato from the well. Immediately he questioned us as to whether we knew anything about how the potatoes had gotten into the well. Both of us denied that we knew anything about it, having already threatened my sister and aunt not to tell on us. As more potatoes began to appear the girls broke and told all.

Instead of a strapping, Daddy made us draw all of the rotten potatoes from the water in the well and then to draw all of the water from the well so that fresh could come into it. If you have never tried to draw a well of water dry, I would urge you to forget it and I would warn you not to play "Bombs Away" in a well.

MISCELLANEOUS

As I stated above, some of my experiences cannot be neatly fitted into a cubbyhole. The following stories are part of my life in MY TOWN and are unique to me. Still each of you probably share similar experiences.

DISCIPLINE

Parents who discipline their children today tend to follow Dr. Spock or a theory of child discipline as preached in some psychology book. Many young parents fail to realize that discipline does not ruin a child, but assists the child to grow up and adjust to the adult world. Not enough parents of today follow the biblical admonition, "Spare the rod and spoil the child." Parents in MY TOWN not only believed that saying, but also practiced it. I remember vividly two cases when my parents practiced it on me and on my sister.

Once as a young boy of six or seven I got into an argument with my sister over a small rocker which belonged to her. Now my Daddy had listened to us fuss for several minutes and finally his patience wore thin. He said to me, "J.D., if you do not stop arguing with your sister, I am going to take a belt and blister you." Well, as usual, I had to get in another couple of words. Despite my protestations that it was really my sister's fault that we were arguing, my Daddy had taken all he could and he grabbed me and his belt. My Daddy is a big man who swung a mean belt. After several whacks, he stopped; but my wailing did not. I complained, "Daddy, you have blistered me. I cannot sit down." He responded, "If you do not shut up, I will burst the blister." Again, I had to get in the last word so Daddy reached for the belt with one hand and me with the other. Sure enough he broke the blister. I had to eat from the mantle for a week or so. From then on when my Daddy told me to shut up, I quickly shut my mouth.

The other time I was disciplined which sticks so clearly in my mind concerned another argument between my sister and me. The discipline this time was administered by my Mother. We lived in a house on Fourth Street in EAST MY TOWN and we had to heat with a wood burning stove. In order to get the fire started, we used "lidard" (lightwood, the proper spelling) splinters. These were slender pieces of wood which came from the heart of a pine tree or stump. The turpentine in them made them ideal for beginning a fire, but also caused them to have a large number of splinters which would stick in a person's hands. Well, my sister and I began arguing in earnest about some trivial matter. Mother listened as long as she could stand it, then she took two of those "lidard" splinters and handed one to each of us. She said, "Now I want you to hit each other with these splinters as long as you can. If you stop, I will belt you." At first, we relished the idea of being able to vent our anger on one another. Soon the excitement evaporated and we collapsed in each others arms, protesting to Mother that we did not want to hit each other. She agreed that we could stop and admonished that we would have to repeat the performance if we argued again. The lesson lasted for several days.

Today if a parent used such tactics, children would resort to seeking some lawyer to sue their parents for child abuse. We never dreamed of such a thing because we knew that our parents had our best interests at heart. All of our beltings were more than justly deserved. As a matter of fact, we probably escaped several that we should have gotten.

CHEWING GUM

One of the banes of my life has been chewing gum. Today I refuse to chew the stuff, but I am still cursed by it. If I go into a parking lot and someone has disposed of a wad of it by spitting it onto the ground, my feet will gravitate toward it like a nail to a magnet. I invariably wind up having to scrape it from the bottom of my shoes. But without that reason, I have had enough bad luck with gum that I have sworn off for life.

Like all kids I loved to do the forbidden. One of the cardinal rules in our school was that a student could not chew gum in class. Of course, all of us tried to get by that rule on more than one occasion. It was not unusual to find several wads of chewed gum stuck under the top of a desk where some student had tried to avoid being caught by a teacher. Once I had just put a fresh stick of gum in my mouth and had not really gotten to savor it when the teacher called upon me to answer a question, I could not swallow the gum fast enough so the teacher caught me. I had to write that I would not chew gum in the class one hundred times. It broke me of the habit for a short time, but it did not cure me.

Another time I got into a fight with a classmate who was chewing gum and in the melee his gum wound up in my hair. I had a hard time explaining to my parents how I had gotten gum in my hair. I knew that if I told the truth I would get a whipping for fighting. I made up some excuse about someone sneaking up behind me and putting it in my hair.

One thing which helped turn me against chewing gum occurred when I was on the junior high basketball team. In practice one day, I put a piece of Juicy Fruit in my mouth. I had to run up and down the court rather quickly for several minutes. By the time I had made four or five trips up and down the court that gum had become so sweet in my mouth that it made me sick. From that day I have never chewed Juicy Fruit gum.

The straw which finally broke the camel's back occurred due to my carelessness. When I would want a change in the gum I chewed, I would buy a packet of Chicklets. This was a candy coated gum which came in a box rather than in a package. Once when I was home I knew that Mother had some Chicklets in her medicine cabinet. Without watching what I was doing I grabbed the first box and popped a couple of pieces of the candy into my mouth. What I had not noticed was that the box was a box of Feen-A-Mint. I did not discover my mistake for several hours until I began to have to make some quick trips outside to our two-holer (we lived in the country and had a four room house with a path). After that experience I decided that I could live the remainder of my life without chewing gum!

THE CHIMNEY

One of the proudest moments in my Daddy's life came when he and Mother bought a farm west of MY TOWN. He immediately set about to convince us that we should move to the country. Since we had lived in town all of our lives, we were not too crazy about leaving all of our friends and the convenience of living in town. Finally, we gave in and plans were made to move us to the country. It was a move which we came to love.

The house sat upon a hill side in such a manner that it was hidden from the road, but so that anyone sitting on the porch could see the cars as they traveled down the road. When we first moved out to the country, the road was not paved. In wet weather it became something of a feat to make it home in a car without getting stuck in the mud. Not too long after we moved, however, the county paved the road.

Our house had four rooms, a front porch, a back porch, a well on the back porch, and an outhouse. I joke with my friends about living in a house with four rooms and a path. In one of the front rooms there was a fire-place, but the other front room did not have one. My daddy decided to build a chimney on the outside of that room so that we could put a wood stove in it.

Daddy secured all of the materials that he needed to build the chimney. After checking around with some brick layers, he decided that he would build it himself. Now my Daddy is the most patient person I know, but occasionally someone can get his goat. He set to work on the chimney. He got on top of the house and hung a plumb line from it to the ground. Having done that he set about laying the bricks. Working carefully to keep the plumb line straight, he added layer after layer of bricks. One hot summer day as he worked on the chimney, George Johnson, a neighbor, came by to see Daddy. George backed away and looked at the chimney. He said, "Marvin, you sure have made that chimney crooked." That was the remark that got Daddy's goat. He snapped, "George, if you don't like the (expletive deleted) thing, you don't have to look at it." George Johnson never said another word to Daddy about his chimney. It was crooked, but Daddy had built it and he didn't want anyone criticizing it.

THE SILO AND TANK

In these days of satellite television where we can see events happening in remote parts of the globe, the following story could not have taken place. It did occur many years ago in MY TOWN.

The depression of 1929 caused several changes in the lives of families in MY TOWN. Many able bodied young men found that there was no job to be had. When President Roosevelt started the Civilian Conservation Corps, several young men from MY TOWN joined. It meant that they could earn some money to send back to their families. This allowed them to travel and to see things and meet people that they never knew before. Those who remained at home were confined to a limited knowledge of the outside world. They had the <u>Montgomery Advertiser</u> to read, but many did not bother to read anything but the comics and sports. Few people in MY TOWN owned radios. Any exposure to outside culture was accidental in most cases.

One of my uncles managed to get over to Mississippi during this period. While over there he met and married a lovely young lady from a farm family in the Columbus area. This young lady had grown up on a farm which had silos on it. After the marriage my uncle brought his new bride home to MY TOWN, where she was welcomed by the entire family.

In MY TOWN stood two water tanks. These had stood as a symbol of it as long as I can remember and they dominated the downtown area. I suppose everybody just assumed that anyone would know what they were.

One day while my uncle was busy, another uncle decided to show his new sister-in-law the downtown area of MY TOWN. As they approached the water tanks, my aunt asked, "What are those? Silos?"

My startled uncle said, "Those are water tanks. What are silos?" Country met city. Each had a time trying to explain what the other did not know. The retelling of the misadventure resulted in many a laugh for my family.

WARM IT UP

Today's customer is protected against obsolete products because the government requires that a date be stamped on each item. This means that goods that are perishable as well as those that appear to be non-perishable cannot be sold after their expiration date. Smart shoppers always check to insure that they are getting fresh products. It has not always been possible to do that as can be seen from a story that occurred in MY TOWN.

In MY TOWN a local businessman operated a bakery. Since there were not enough businesses within the confines of MY TOWN to support the bakery, he hired deliverymen to deliver his bread throughout the region. The lucky deliverymen got the more populated routes. The less lucky ones got the rural routes which contained widely separated country stores. This made the job rather lonely, since one would have to load his truck early and deliver the bread to the stores in the morning.

One of these deliverymen, whom I shall not name because of the nature of the story, decided that he was in need of assistance on the weekend. Once while eating at the Snack Shop, he mentioned his desire to hire a young boy to travel his route with him on the weekend to assist him. My Mother suggested that her younger brother who was living with her would welcome the job.   As a result, my uncle began his work life as an assistant deliveryman for the local bakery.

One weekend when my uncle had to miss his job for some reason or another, I was pressed into filling in for him. I met the deliveryman at the appointed place, assisted him in loading his truck, and joined him as we set out on the route.

During the first part of the route, the deliveryman filled the requirements of his customers with fresh bread. He would replace the two or three day old bread which had not been sold with freshly baked bread. Obviously he knew his customers and their sales record. As time and distance went by, our supply of fresh bread began to dwindle. Toward the end of the route, the deliveryman entered a small rural grocery store. The owner told him to "warm up" a couple of loaves of bread. The deliveryman knew that meant to exchange them for fresh bread, but he went with me to the back of the truck and since the supply of fresh bread had dwindled until there was none left he "warmed up" the bread by running a match under it. He grinned and said, "I warmed it up." The poor storekeeper got the same loaves of bread that he had seen go out of his store and never knew the difference. It was a dirty trick, but there was no way to prove it.

SNIPE HUNTING

Almost every society has its ritual of passage by which a young man moves from being considered a kid by his elders to becoming a young adult. In some Indian societies this was accomplished by placing a teenager in the woods with the necessary weapons to survive a specified period of time. In others it was marked by the young man's killing of his first buck deer.

In MY TOWN, one of the rituals of passage was snipe hunting. I suppose that almost every young man there either participated in or was told about the ritual. To carry out the process, there had to be a young man, one or more adults, and an empty "croaker" sack. Once these ingredients had been assembled the ritual could begin.

A beautiful, warm autumn night with a full moon would be picked for the expedition. The adults would take the young man into the woods. When they had found the suitable spot, they told the young man that snipe had been seen in abundance in the area. They then told him that his job was to stay in the spot where they placed him and to hold the sack open while they went out and drove the snipe into the bag. Upon placing the youth with the open bag where they wanted him, the adults would scatter into the woods. As they moved around, they made noises for awhile and then moved further and further away from the young man. Finally, they would disappear and return home. The idea was that after an hour or so the young man would catch on that he had been left "holding the bag" and would fold it and return home.

One night the ritual backfired on the tricksters. They took a friend of mine into the woods, told him that he was to stand and hold the bag open while they drove the snipe into it, then they left. They returned home, laughing about how they had tricked the young man. They sat around for an hour laughing and talking while waiting on the young man to catch on and return so that they could make fun of him. Two hours went by and no youth; three hours and no sign was seen of the young man. Finally, about midnight, they began to worry that something had happened to the lad. They returned to the spot where they had left the boy and was greeted by him with, " Hi, I guess you guys just couldn't scare up any snipes tonight."

WATERMELON STEALIN'

Summertime in MY TOWN meant watermelons. Farmers tried to see if they could get melons to ripen by July fourth; seldom did they make it. From about the second or third week in July, however, there were plenty of melons. Nothing was prettier in the eyes of teenagers than a field loaded with watermelons of all shapes and colors. There were those with the deep green skins, others with lighter green, others with streaks of black running in a pattern around the melon, and their shapes ranged from those perfectly round ones to knotty ones to long slender melons.

One thing on which farmers could count was at least one group of teenagers raiding his patch for several "free" melons at least once during the year. These "purchases" were usually done under the cover of night with great fear and trepidation. Seldom did we hear of anyone getting blasted by a farmer's shotgun, but the fear was always there. Because of that fear the plan of attack was to post a watchman and to send several of the biggest and fastest members of the group into the field to "capture" the prize of as many watermelons as the group wanted.

One night, following a cheerleading practice, a group of us planned a "raid" on a local farmer's watermelon patch. We never thought that we were in reality "stealing"; that is never until Carolyn Dunn, now Carolyn Totty, spoke up. She admonished us with the fact that her uncle, J. T. Jones, was a farmer who raised watermelons and that it was hard work. She continued to inform us that she would not take part in our "raid" and that we were stealing. Carolyn's "pep-talk" did not deter our activity, but she did absent herself from it.

Upon the completion of practice, all of us, except Carolyn, got into a car and went to the designated patch. We "lifted" a couple of melons and headed for the old train depot. Under the safety of that old building we broke open the melons and began to eat. The more I ate, the more I thought of Carolyn's speech. After a few bites I felt that I was going to choke on watermelon which would have been a hard thing to do. From that time on watermelon lost its appeal to me, so that today I refuse to eat it. I guess her speech awoke my conscience because I never raided another watermelon patch.

DIRTY TRICKS

Words take on different meanings at various times in history. Ever since Richard Nixon's campaigns for the Presidency, the term "dirty tricks' has been associated with political shenanigans. The term meant something else to the people of MY TOWN. It referred to the good-natured pranks which they frequently played on each other. Few people were exempt from being either a perpetrator or a victim.

Two of the biggest pranksters in MY TOWN were my father and Mr. Charlie Ashurst. Both of them worked for the company store, Mr. Charlie was the butcher and my father worked in several different capacities there.

There was always a gang of individuals hanging around the store from time to time. Many of these people became the butt of jokes which the two pranksters would pull. One young Black boy who frequented the store and who did odd jobs around it from time to time was named Reese. I do not know if he had any other name or not, since the only thing I ever heard him called was Reese. He was a very jolly person who seemed to get along with everybody. I suppose his biggest fault, if one can call it a fault, was that he tended to trust everyone, which often got him into trouble. Even after tricks had been played on him, he still accepted whatever anyone told him.

One day, Mr. Charlie and my Dad decided to play a really rotten trick on Reese. Daddy set Reese up by telling him that Mr. Charlie was the best detective alive, even better than Dick Tracy. That really caused Reese to sit up and take notice. To prove his point my father told Reese to stand and watch as he hid an egg on his person and to see if Mr. Charlie could find it. He placed the egg in a pocket of the raincoat he was wearing. Obviously, he and Mr. Charlie had made an agreement whereby Mr. Charlie would go through the pretext of hunting for the egg and finally finding it in the pocket.

Reese was fascinated by this feat. When Daddy proposed that he hide the egg on Reese, he was more than willing to have it done. My father placed the egg under Reese's ball cap. Mr. Charlie came out and began a body search of Reese. The more he looked and appeared to be baffled the wider became Reese's grin that he and my Dad had pulled one over on the world's greatest detective. Finally, as if giving up in desperation, Mr. Charlie slapped Reese on the head saying, "I give up!" Reese's joy was dispelled by the dripping of the egg onto his head and face. At last, he realized he had been had. He took the joke with his usual good humor. To soften the blow the two pranksters bought him lunch.

QUILTING

Quilting is an art that is about to become obsolete. Machines and short-cuts that the ladies use today are making quilting as I observed it in my youth disappear. I suppose that the way my grandmother quilted was much more work than the way it is done today. I do know that she never received the prices for her quilts that the ladies who quilt today receive. For me my grandmother's quilting was something special.

My grandmother would spend several weeks or months sewing scraps of material together to make a quilt top, using small pieces of cloth that were left over from her other sewing. Many times she worked a design into the quilt, such as a star, a triangle, or some other shape. This sewing she did by hand or on the sewing machine and it did not interest me, but when she finished the top I really became interested.

My grandfather helped my grandmother get her quilting frames out and set up. I was always fascinated by those quilting frames. They consisted of two saw-horse looking pieces on each end. Down the sides would be two long pieces with a number of holes punched in them.

When the frames were brought out, it would be determined as to how far apart the end pieces would be placed. This was decided by the length of the quilt top. The top would be stretched from one end to the other and also along the two sides pieces. It would be secured by clamps. Once this had been done, my grandmother would get some cotton and begin to spread it out over the top which had been placed in the quilting frame upside down.

When the cotton was completely spread, my grandmother would invite several of her friends in and they would have a quilting bee. With deft and nimble fingers these ladies would stitch the backing of the quilt to the top, forcing the cotton to stay in place.

Obviously, I was not interested in the details of quilt making. As a boy I found these quilting frames to be interesting for another reason. I always had an active imagination and those frames served me beautifully as a tent into which I could crawl and read my comic books. I read many a comic book, ate several boxes of crackers, and listened to many a tale while hidden in my "secret tent."

SCOUTING

Most boys dream of the time that they can join the Boy Scouts and the boys in MY TOWN were no exception. As we approached the age where we became eligible for the Cub Scouts, we began plotting which troop we would try to join. As I neared that magic age, I realized that my choice was a Cub Scout troop run by Mrs. Capers Joiners and sponsored by First Baptist Church.

At last my invitation to join the Cub Scout troop known as the Wolf Pack came. I proudly marched to that first meeting and was informed of what I had to do to take the oath to become a Cub Scout. I faithfully followed all of the assigned procedures and was enrolled as a member of Wolf Pack. I returned home happier than a kid who had his tonsils removed and has been told that he can eat all of the ice cream he wants.

I entered the house shouting to my Mother and Daddy about my being a Cub Scout. I handed them a list of items which comprised the official Cub Scout uniform. They looked at each other realizing that to outfit me would strain severely their budget, but seeing the glow in my face they made a vow to make the sacrifice.

Mother took me to Clower's Clothing Store which was the official headquarters for scouting uniforms. I beamed proudly as the lady measured me for my shirt, short pants, scarf, and cap which comprised the official uniform. I also wheedled an official scout knife from my parents. As I left that store, wearing my new outfit, I felt like I owned the world. I am sure that my parents were proud of me, although they had had to skimp on other items in their budget to provide for my pleasure.

The next couple of meetings went fine. I attended and began working on my merit badges. I wanted so badly to succeed and rise through the ranks so that when I reached the proper age I could become a full-fledged Boy Scout. I earned a couple of badges and felt really good about my scouting experience.

After about the third or fourth meeting, Wayne Joiner, Mrs. Joiner's youngest son who was not old enough to join the troop but obviously had to be there since it was at his home, and I got into a fight. I do not remember what started it, probably I smarted off about something or other. Nevertheless Wayne and I had a donnybrook. I do not remember how it turned out, again he probably got the best of it.

I trudged slowly homeward. I knew that I had a lot of explaining to do for I had succeeded in tearing my shirt in the fight. As I entered the house, I began giving my Mother my excuses for the fight. Much to my surprise she did not take a belt to me; she provided a much harsher punishment. She said, "Your father and I did not spend our good money for you to go to Cub Scouts to learn to fight, therefore you will not go back." I am sure that I cried and pleaded, but to no avail. I eventually sold my uniform and my scouting days were finished. Fighting did not pay for me.

HOME BREW

The persons involved in this story shall go nameless to protect them and especially to keep me from getting something that I have not had in a long time--a belting. The events in the story are real, but I do not want to embarrass the parties involved.

Once during World War II or shortly thereafter, a certain fellow in MY TOWN decided he would try to make some home brew. I do not really know the reason behind his actions for he did not drink. At any rate, the decision was made and the ingredients were gathered.

Only one problem remained--the kids. In order to dispose of them the decision to make the home brew was postponed until a Saturday afternoon when they were herded off to their western movie. Problem solved!

After the departure of the kids, the gentleman and his spouse brought forth the necessary materials and began their nefarious operations. The bottles were scrubbed, the mash mixed, and the cooking process begun. Now since I was not privy to the process and have not learned how to make home-brew, I can only report that the two did what was necessary to turn the mash into the finished product. As soon as the brew cooled, the couple bottled it in the clean bottles. After bottling it, they placed it in a couple of boxes. In order to keep it from the kids, they decided to hide the bottled brew under their bed where the kids were forbidden to look.

Having completed their rather dubious task, they went to town to pick up the kids. Upon the return of the kids, family life went on as usual. Each one went about his or her assigned task. The boys milked the cows and the girls helped with supper. Since it was the fall of the year, the kids played outside for several hours before bedtime, which finally came. The family retired for the night as usual.

Sunday morning dawned beautifully. The family arose and tended to their chores. After they finished them, they sat down to breakfast. As the syrup was being passed, a sound like a gunshot occurred in the parents' bedroom. A knowing look passed between the father and the mother. Moments later a second shot sounded and then another and another. The adults sprang up from the table and headed for their bedroom. Naturally the kids followed. As the father pulled the cases from under the bed, another sound erupted from the case. Home-brew began to run out onto the floor. Quickly, the man took the case to the back porch and returned for the second case. Once he had removed them, the adults began to explain to the kids what had happened. It seems that in their haste to finish their project before the return of the kids from the movies, they had bottled the brew while it was still green. Over night it had fermented and blew the caps from the bottles the next morning. That ended the home brewing escapade!

CONVICTS

My parents taught us kids to never lie to them. Their method was simply that if they caught us in a lie, we could count on a good belting. You would be surprised how effective that method can be! Anyway, most of the time, we followed their admonition. Once, however, I remember a time when my uncle and I lied and I think, or at least we were led to believe, got away with it.

As my uncle and I got into high school there was a lot of pressure on us go try cigarettes. Being boys, we decided that we should learn to smoke. Now my parents had told us that smoking was a bad habit and was harmful to our health. We had, nonetheless, to try it. The question was how to fool my parents.

One of the chores that my uncle and I had was milking the cows. This meant that early in the morning and in the late afternoon, we would have to go to the barn to perform these chores. It also provided us some time during which we escaped supervision by an adult. We decided that this was the perfect time and place to cultivate our smoking habit.

Now I always thought it more manly to smoke a pipe than cigarettes, but a pipe would be much more risky to try to hide. My uncle and I therefore settled upon Camel cigarettes. We sneaked a couple of packs to the barn where we could smoke them while we were milking. We did this for several weeks. During that time, I found that I did not like the taste of cigarettes, but I was not about to let my uncle out smoke me.

One day, Daddy was working in the hay loft and found our packs of Camels where we had hid them. He came to the house and confronted us in Mother's presence. With as straight a face a we could muster, we denied that we knew anything about the Camels or their origin. Luckily for us, there had been rumors of a couple of escaped convicts in our neighborhood. My uncle and I immediately surmised that those convicts must have sneaked into our barn to escape the law and that they must have brought their Camels with them. Neither of us stopped to think that the last thing that an escaped convict would leave behind would be his cigarettes. Daddy looked at Mother and a knowing wink passed between them. Daddy said, "You boys are right. It must have been those convicts, so you had better be careful when you go to the barn to milk." Grateful for our reprieve, we assured Daddy that we would keep a close lookout for them. That experience broke our smoking habit for awhile and I never did develop a taste for cigarettes, so I can be grateful to two nonexistent convicts for aiding me in becoming a non-smoker.

LIMING

There are things that one does out of ignorance, others out of devilment, and others which seem to blend the two elements. I was once caught in a situation where I did something out of ignorance that turned out to be very cruel and extremely dangerous. In the summer the creeks in the countryside around MY TOWN could get pretty low from a lack of rainfall. Near my home was one of the major creeks that flowed into the river south of MY TOWN. All along the creek were farms containing cattle.

266

One summer, rain was extremely scarce. A relative of mine came to my house one day and suggested that we take some lime and go to the creek to fish. Ignorance is no excuse in the eyes of the law, but I did not know that it was illegal nor did I realize how cruel it was when I agreed to go.

I put on an old pair of blue jeans, a white tee-shirt, and a pair of rubber boots. I placed the boots on the inside of my pants legs. (The importance of this will emerge shortly.) After I was properly dressed, we set out for the creek.

The idea was to find a pot hole into which the creek had ceased to flow, but which still had enough water for the fish to live. Once we had located such a hole, we poured lime into it. The lime depleted the oxygen and the fish would come to the top for air. At that point we would clubbed the fish into a state of unconsciousness and lifted them from the water. Having depleted the supply of fish in one hole, we moved to the next until we felt like we had "caught" all of the fish we wanted,

As I think back on that experience, I realize two gross wrongs on my part. First, there must be no more horrible way for any life to end than from a lack of oxygen. The barbarity of the act did not register on me at that time, but as I had time to ponder it I became really ashamed of having participated in it. The second wrong was the danger into which we placed all of the cattle which drank from that creek once it began to flow again, or even as they came to the pot holes to drink. I never knew of any cattle that perished because of our act, but that does not excuse us.

Now lest you think that wrongdoers get away without any punishment, let me remind you of the rubber boots. As I stated, I placed them on the inside of my pant legs. These boots did not lace up, but were rather loose fitting. As my pants legs became wet, they began to stick to my legs and that caused the rubber boots to rub the area of my legs just below the knee raw. For those of you who do not know how lime affects open wounds, let me tell you that you do not want to know. For several weeks, I walked around with raw sores on the back of my legs. I vowed that the only way I would catch fish from then on would be on a rod and reel!

THE PANTHER

Practical jokes were a fact of life in MY TOWN. Since there was no television and since few people sat around listening to the radio, many tended to dream up pranks to play on one another. By today's standards some of them would be thought cruel and dangerous, but they were not considered so by those who dreamed them up and by those upon whom they were played. One of the best, in my memory, concerned one that my father pulled on our cook, Pearl, and our neighbor's cook, Molly.

Frequently, when the people in MY TOWN did not have to work a double shift in the mill, they would sit around in the evening talking and telling tales. One summer my father began to tell a tale about a panther which had escaped from a circus in Montgomery. He always made sure that Pearl heard the story, which was backed by the rest of the family. After a week or so, Pearl just knew that panther had had time to come from Montgomery to MY TOWN.

In the backyard of our house was a big mulberry tree from which Daddy had hung us a tire swing. One evening, after the supper dishes had been washed and put away, Pearl and Molly went to our neighbor's backyard where they sat in straight chairs and talked. All of the family, except me, had gathered to the front porch and were talking. Since I was recovering from scarlet fever, I was isolated in a backroom.

Shortly after dark, my father came to the back of the house and told me to ease over to the window. He slipped out the back door, climbed the tree without the cooks becoming suspicious, and pulled the tire swing up the tree. As he got the swing to the top, he overheard the ladies commenting that they had heard some noise like an animal climbing a tree but they dismissed it as a cat.

Pearl said to Molly, "Reckon that is that panther?" That became the focus of their conversation for the next several minutes. At the point where Daddy thought they had convinced themselves that it might be the panther, he dropped the tire swing and screamed like a woman which was how he had described the sound of a panther to the women.

Both women bolted from their chairs. As a matter of fact, Molly grabbed her chair and still holding onto it jumped a porch swing which hung on our neighbor's backporch, she was so frightened. Pearl came running around the house screaming, "Mista Marvin, come quick that panther is 'round here and he's 'bout to get me and Molly."

In the meantime, my father scampered down the tree and ran through the house to try to beat Pearl to the front. As he came out the front door, Pearl begged him to go see about the panther. He told her that he would, if she would go with him and show him where she had seen the panther. She absolutely refused.

To make the story more believable, the next morning my father eased out of the house and took a fork and scratched the ground so that it looked like an animal had been there. For weeks after Pearl and Molly would not sit in the backyard at night. Despite a confession from my father and other members of the family, Pearl and Molly never believed that it was a trick and remained convinced that they had barely escaped being eaten by a panther.

GOODBYE

I invited you to visit MY TOWN with me. I promised to introduce you to some of the people, to mention some of the places, to tell about some of the institutions and to share some of the history of MY TOWN. In the course of our visit you have shared with me many memories that have been very pleasant to recall.

Many of the people whom you have met were not heroes nor shakers and movers within MY TOWN. Even though these individuals are not mentioned in the history of MY TOWN, they were and are a part of its history. No community can exist without all of the people who live in it. There is no man on earth from· whom we cannot learn something.

Changes occurred to many of the places which we recalled. The teacherage no longer exists. The school has undergone numerous changes. The downtown area has ceased to be as vital as it was. The theaters have closed.

On the list goes, so MY TOWN has gone the way of the passenger pigeon.

The forms of entertainment which captivated me as a kid no longer relate to the young people of today. They do not seem to have the ability to amuse themselves like we did. The games which we played seem to have disappeared from today's scene. It worries me that so many young people do not get a chance to develop their imagination like we did. They are not as creative in their amusements.

MY TOWN and the people who lived in it furnished me with the necessary values to guide me through life. Those are the values, people, and events which I will cherish and continue to cultivate the remainder of my life.

As I leave you I want to challenge you to remember that while MY TOWN no longer exists, YOUR TOWN does. It will become to you what you make of it. It can provide you with values which will sustain you throughout your life. It can furnish you with fond memories which will arm you for the rest of your life. The greatest danger is that you will go through life without thinking about the values and the people who mean the most to you as you live in YOUR TOWN. This is the tragedy of too many people who live in today's fast-paced world!

273